WordPerfect® 6.1 for Windows® Essentials

Linda Hefferin
Elgin Community College
&
Laura Acklen

QUE
COLLEGE

WordPerfect 6.1 for Windows Essentials

Library of Congress Catalog No.: 94-69258

ISBN: 0-7897-0104-9

98 97 96 95   4 3 2 1

Interpretation of the printing code: the rightmost double-digit number is the year of the book's printing; the rightmost single-digit number, the number of the book's printing. For example, a printing code of 95-1 shows that the first printing of the book occurred in 1995.

Screens reproduced in this book were created using Collage Plus from Inner Media, Inc., Hollis, NH.

WordPerfect 6.1 for Windows Essentials is based on WordPerfect 6.1 for Windows.

Publisher: David P. Ewing

Associate Publisher: Paul Boger

Publishing Manager: Chris Katsaropoulos

Marketing Manager: Susan J. Dollman

Managing Editor: Sheila Cunningham

Production Editor: Beth Hux

Book Designer: Paula Carroll

Acquisitions Coordinator: Elizabeth D. Brown

Production Team: Claudia Bell, Anne Dickerson, Chad Dressler, Karen Gregor, Aren Howell, Beth Lewis, Michael Thomas, Scott Tullis

About the Authors

Linda Hefferin is a full-time professor in the Business Division at Elgin Community College in Elgin, Illinois. In addition to teaching WordPerfect and Microsoft Word, she teaches a variety of other types of applications including spreadsheet, graphics, database, and personal information management. Linda is a Certified Novell® Instructor and author or co-author of several other Que books.

Dedicated to TMD

Laura Acklen is an independent author and instructor located in Austin, Texas. She has been training and supporting computer users in DOS and Windows products since 1986. Laura has written over 15 student manuals and instructor guides for the national training company, Productivity Point International. She is the author of Que's *WordPerfect 6.0 SureSteps* and co-author of *Oops! WordPerfect...What To Do When Things Go Wrong*. She is also a contributing author of *Using WordPerfect Version 6 for Windows*, Special Edition, *Using WordPerfect Version 6.1 for Windows*, Special Edition, and the revision author for *Windows QuickStart*, 3.11 Edition. Her most recent project is Que's *First Look at Windows 95*.

To all my "sisters"—Becky, Kelly, Patty, Lynn, and Sharon

Acknowledgments

Que College is grateful for the assistance provided by the following reviewers: Mike Miller, Kansas State University, and Allan Koeningsburg, LaGuardia Community College. And thank you to our technical editor, Tish Nye.

Preface

Que College is the educational publishing imprint of Macmillan Computer Publishing, the world's leading computer book publisher. Macmillan Computer Publishing books have taught over 20 million people how to be productive with their computers.

This expertise in producing high-quality computer tutorial and reference books is also evident in every Que College title we publish. The same tried and true authoring and product development process that makes Macmillan Computer Publishing books bestsellers is used to ensure that every Que College textbook has the most accurate and most up-to-date information. Experienced and respected college instructors write and review every manuscript to provide class-tested pedagogy. Quality assurance editors check every keystroke and command in Que College books to ensure that instructions are clear and precise.

Above all, Macmillan Computer Publishing and, in turn, Que College, has years of experience at meeting the learning demands of computer users in business and at home. This "real-world" experience means Que College textbooks help students understand how the skills they learn will be applied and why these skills are important.

The "Essentials" of Hands-On Learning

Thank you for using the *Essentials* series in your classroom. This collection of hands-on tutorials is designed to be used separately or as computer lab application modules to accompany *Computers in Your Future* by Marilyn Meyer and Roberta Baber of Fresno City College. The four-color modules, presented in a project-driven chapter format, cover the fundamental elements of each application. The tutorials are designed for a broad spectrum of majors, although the business case problems contained in the end-of-chapter material also make them suitable for use in schools of business. Each *Essentials* volume is four-color throughout, and sized at 8 1/2" x 11" for maximum screen shot visibility.

Project Objectives list what your student will do and learn from this project.

Why Would I Do This? shows your student why this material is essential.

Step-by-Step Tutorials simplify the procedure with large screen shots, captions, and annotations.

If you have problems... anticipates common pitfalls and advises your student accordingly.

Inside Stuff provides tips and shortcuts for more effective applications.

Key Terms are highlighted in the text and defined in the margin when they first appear.

Jargon Watch offers a layman's view of "technobabble" in easily understandable terms.

Concepts Sidebars showcase intriguing topics normally covered in the Concepts course, and serve to integrate pertinent material with Meyer/Baber's *Computers in Your Future*.

Checking Your Skills provides True/False, Multiple Choice, Completion, and Screen Labeling exercises.

Applying Your Skills contains hands-on case studies that test students' critical thinking skills and ability to apply what they've learned. The *On Your Own* case study lets students use their newly learned skills in a personally oriented application. *Brief Cases* test the student's skills in a business environment.

The Essentials series covers the following applications in both Windows 3.1 and Windows 95 versions:

Word 6 for Windows

1-2-3 Release 5 for Windows

Excel 5 for Windows

Access 2 for Windows

Microsoft Office

Works 3 for Windows

Lotus 1-2-3 Release 5 for Windows

Paradox 5 for Windows

Quattro Pro 6 for Windows

The series also includes manuals on Internet, Personal Computing, Windows 3.1, and Windows 95.

An Instructor's Manual contains suggested curriculum guides for courses of varying lengths, teaching tips, answers to questions appearing in the **Checking Your Skills** and **Applying Your Skills** sections, test questions (and answers), additional projects, and a data disk with files for the text's step-by-step tutorials. The Instructor's Manual is available by request to teachers upon adoption of any of the ***Essentials*** manuals. Please contact your local representative or write to us on school letterhead at Macmillan Computer Publishing, 201 W. 103rd Street, Indianapolis, IN 46290-1097, Attn: S. Dollman.

The Que College commitment to the educational market demands that we listen and respond to the needs of professors and students. At Que College, our most important partners are you, the end users. To help us continue to provide you with the best in computer education, we look to you for continual feedback. If you have any questions or comments regarding this product, or are interested in acting as a reviewer on future endeavors, please write to Chris Katsaropoulos, Publishing Manager, Macmillan Computer Publishing, 201 W. 103rd Street, Indianapolis, IN 46290-1097.

Que College
Publishing for tomorrow...*today*.

Table of Contents at a Glance

Table of Contents

Project 1

Getting Started with WordPerfect for Windows

In this project, you learn how to

- Start WordPerfect for Windows
- Learn the WordPerfect Screen
- Use Menus and Dialog Boxes
- Customize WordPerfect
- Get Help
- Exit WordPerfect

Why Would I Do This?

Personal computer
A stand-alone computer equipped with all the system, utility, and application software and input/output devices needed to perform one or more tasks.

Word processing software is the most common application software used on *personal computers*. It's estimated that some form of word processing software is installed on 95 percent of the personal computers in use. Word processing software is easy to use, and nearly everyone has some reason to use it. As you work through the projects in this book, you will discover why word processing software such as WordPerfect for Windows has become so popular.

Document
A file containing created work, such as a report, memo, or worksheet.

WordPerfect for Windows lets you create, modify, and format *documents* quickly and easily. In this project, you begin learning how WordPerfect works and what you can do with WordPerfect by starting the software and taking a tour of the WordPerfect screen. You learn how to customize WordPerfect, and you learn how to use the Help system—an invaluable tool when you are just starting to use the program. After becoming familiar with WordPerfect, you learn how to exit the program successfully.

Lesson 1: Starting WordPerfect for Windows

The first thing you need to know about WordPerfect for Windows is how to start the software. Because you start WordPerfect for Windows from the Windows Program Manager, you must open Windows before you go any further.

Starting WordPerfect is simple to do—it's as easy as starting your car Try starting WordPerfect now.

To Start WordPerfect for Windows

❶ Turn on the computer and monitor.

At this point, most computers display technical information about the computer and the operating software installed on the machine. The computer will probably display the *DOS* prompt (C:\>).

❷ At the DOS prompt C:\>, type WIN, and then press ⌐Enter⌐ to start Windows.

The computer loads Windows, and the Windows Program Manager should appear on-screen as shown in Figure 1.1. (Your screen may look slightly different depending on how Windows is set up on your computer.) The Program Manager indicates that you are in Windows, which means you can now start WordPerfect for Windows.

It's possible that when you turn on your machine, Windows may start automatically, or you may be able to start Windows by using a menu set up for your system. Also, if your machine is part of a network of computers, your start-up procedures may be different.

3 Locate the WordPerfect for Windows icon (see Figure 1.1).

The WordPerfect icon should appear in a *group window* that has a title such as "WPWin 6.1" or "WPWin 6.0." If the WPWin window is not open, open the program *group icon* by double-clicking the icon with the mouse.

WordPerfect for Windows program icon

Figure 1.1
The Windows Program Manager and the WPWin 6.1 group window.

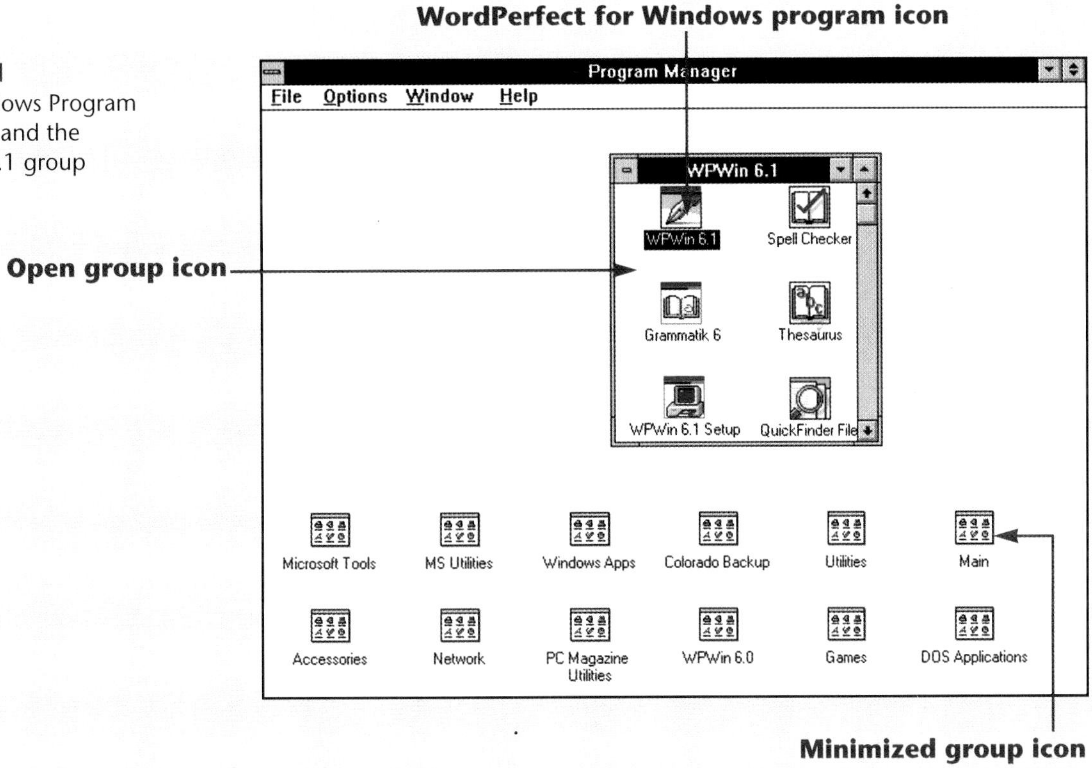

Open group icon

Minimized group icon

If you have problems...

If you can't find the WordPerfect for Windows program icon in an open window and you can't locate the window or the program group icon, try opening other minimized program groups to search for the WordPerfect program icon. The WordPerfect icon may be located in another program group icon that has a title such as "Applications" or "Perfect Office."

continues

To Start WordPerfect for Windows   (continued)

④ Double-click the WordPerfect for Windows program icon.

This action starts the WordPerfect program, and a blank document appears in a window on-screen (see Figure 1.2). Keep this document open to use in the next lesson, where you learn about the WordPerfect for Windows screen.

Figure 1.2
The WordPerfect screen with a blank document.

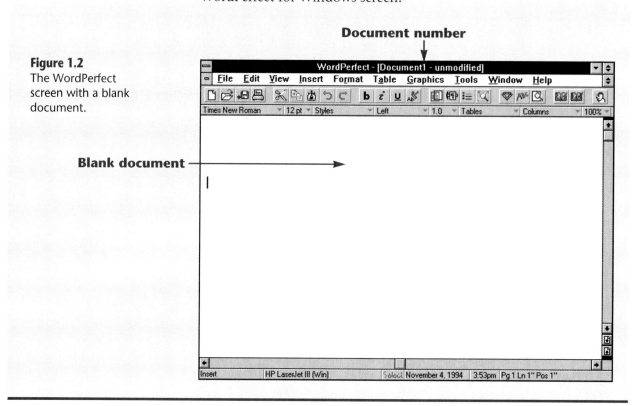

Document number

Blank document

Jargon Watch

You have had to wade through a lot of computer jargon in Lesson 1, which is probably your first experience using WordPerfect. Throughout this book, key terms are defined for you where they are first used, but when a number of these computer terms are introduced in the same lesson, a Jargon Watch box like this one appears to take some of the mystery out of the words.

The term **DOS** stands for Disk Operating System, which acts as a translator between you and the computer. Typing a word at the DOS prompt simply tells the computer what you want to do. For example, when you typed WIN at the DOS prompt, DOS converted that simple command into machine language commands, which told the computer to start the Windows software.

The Windows **Program Manager** does just what the name implies—it manages your programs. Every program has a **program icon**, or picture. Clicking a program icon opens the program that icon represents. Similar program icons are grouped together in **group windows**. When a group window opens, you can see the program icons inside. When a group window is closed (or minimized), it is represented by a **group icon**. (Figure 1.1 shows examples of group windows, group icons, and program icons.)

Lesson 2: Learning the WordPerfect Screen

With WordPerfect for Windows up and running on your computer, it's time to tour the WordPerfect screen. Many elements of the WordPerfect screen may be familiar to you from your work with other Windows programs—elements like the Minimize and Maximize buttons, Control-menus, and scroll bars. Other parts of the screen are features of WordPerfect for Windows that can help you complete your work quickly and efficiently. For example, the Toolbar and Power Bar are convenient tools you use in most of the projects in this book.

Because WordPerfect is a Windows application, it operates under the same rules as the Windows program. For example, each application opens into a *window*, much like the Program Manager window. One difference, however, is that most applications have separate controls for the application window and the document window. Figure 1.3 shows the *Control-menu* and *Minimize/Maximize buttons* on the *title bar* as well as those on the menu bar. The controls on the title bar are for the application window; the controls on the menu bar are for the document window.

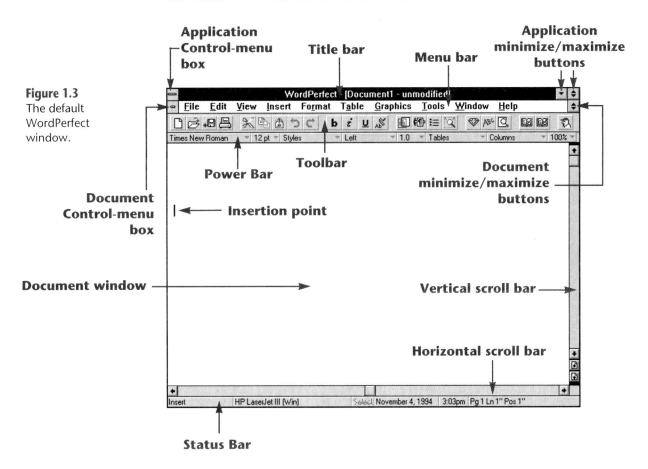

Figure 1.3
The default
WordPerfect
window.

The following table lists the default WordPerfect for Windows 6.1 screen elements and a brief description of each element.

Table 1.1 WordPerfect Screen Elements	
Screen Element	Description
Title bar	Shows the current document number and name, if available. Depending on the mouse position on-screen, a brief description of the screen element displays. When the mouse pointer is pointing to a button on the Toolbar, for example, a brief description of that button appears.
Menu bar	Lists the available main menus and provides access to the pull-down menu system. You can use both the mouse and the keyboard to access the pull-down menus.
Toolbar	A strip of icons that you click with the mouse to access frequently used features. Each icon contains a picture that illustrates that feature.
Power Bar	Accessible only with a mouse, the Power Bar is a strip of buttons representing commonly used menu commands.
Insertion point	Indicates your location on-screen; also indicates where text you type will be inserted into the document window.
Document window	Area where you type, edit, and format your documents.
Vertical scroll bar	Accessible only with a mouse, the vertical scroll bar is used to move up and down in a document.
Horizontal scroll bar	Accessible only with a mouse, the horizontal scroll bar is used to move left and right in a document.
Status Bar	Displays the current feature status, the current printer, whether text is selected or not, the current date and time, the current page number, and the position of the insertion point on the page. Double-click the status bar buttons to change the settings or to access the corresponding dialog box.
Application Control-menu box	Displays the application's Control Menu. Double-click the application's Control-menu box to exit (or close) the application.
Application Minimize/ Maximize buttons	Used to minimize, maximize, and restore the application window.
Document Control-menu box	Displays the document's Control Menu. Double-click the document's Control-menu box to close the document.
Document Minimize/ Maximize buttons	Used to minimize, maximize, and restore the document window.

Refer to Table 1.1 for descriptions of the different screen elements. See Figure 1.3 to help you find your way around the screen. Now try getting to know the elements of the WordPerfect for Windows screen.

To Learn the WordPerfect Screen

❶ Move the mouse pointer to File in the menu bar, and click the left mouse button.

Clicking **F**ile opens the **F**ile menu. Notice that WordPerfect menus look similar to the menus in any Windows program. In WordPerfect, you can open menus and choose commands to perform actions.

❷ Click inside the document window using the mouse.

You can cancel a menu by clicking anywhere in the document window outside of the menu. You can also press (Esc) if you prefer.

❸ Move the mouse pointer to the title bar.

The title bar contains the name of the program and the current document, as well as other standard Window elements such as the Maximize and Minimize buttons (see Figure 1.3).

❹ Move the mouse pointer to the Print icon on the Toolbar.

The third line of the WordPerfect for Windows screen is the Toolbar, which contains a series of *icons*. These icons represent commonly used menu commands. For example, clicking the Print icon is the same as choosing **F**ile, **P**rint.

Notice that when you point to an element on the Toolbar, WordPerfect displays a brief description of that element. These descriptions come in handy when you can't remember what a particular icon does.

❺ Move the mouse pointer to the first button on the Power Bar.

This is the Font Face button, which indicates the currently selected font (see Figure 1.3). The Power Bar uses buttons, rather than icons, to help you perform common tasks. For example, clicking the Font Face button displays a list of available fonts.

❻ Move the mouse pointer into the document window.

Notice how the mouse pointer changes from a left-facing arrow to an object that looks like the letter "I" called an I-beam. Anytime the mouse pointer appears within the document window, it displays as an I-beam.

Icons are small pictures that represent common actions you can perform—generally, the most common things you do using a word processing program. Clicking an icon with the left mouse button selects the action represented by the icon. For example, clicking the Open icon allows you to open an existing file.

Lesson 3: Using Menus and Dialog Boxes

WordPerfect's menu bar, located directly below the title bar, contains menu names; you can open these menus to display WordPerfect commands. You use these commands to do things in WordPerfect, such as editing or formatting text.

In WordPerfect menus, choosing a command that has an ellipsis next to it opens a dialog box. Dialog boxes present a number of options and ask you to choose what you want to do. Try using menus and dialog boxes in WordPerfect now.

To Use Menus and Dialog Boxes

❶ Move the mouse pointer to Format on the menu bar, and click the left mouse button.

The Format menu lists all the commands you can use to format your documents. Once a menu opens, you can click a command with the mouse to select the command.

❷ Drag the mouse down the list to highlight the menu commands; then click Line.

WordPerfect displays a second menu listing the Line Format commands you can choose (see Figure 1.4).

Figure 1.4
The Line Format menu lists the commands to format a line of text.

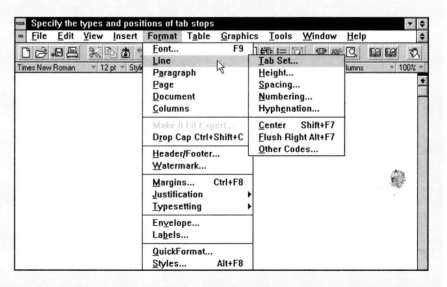

❸ Click inside the document window using the mouse.

4 Choose File from the menu bar.

The **F**ile menu appears. Once a menu opens, you can select a command with the keyboard by using the up and down arrow keys to move through the available menu items. If you prefer to use the keyboard to open the menus, you can press [Alt] plus the underlined key (for example, [Alt] + [F] opens the **F**ile menu.)

The ellipsis (...) following the **O**pen command tells you that a dialog box appears to provide you with further options after you select **O**pen.

5 Press ↓ one time; then press [↵Enter] to choose the Open command.

The Open File dialog box appears (see Figure 1.5).

Figure 1.5
The Open File dialog box is used to open files already saved to a disk.

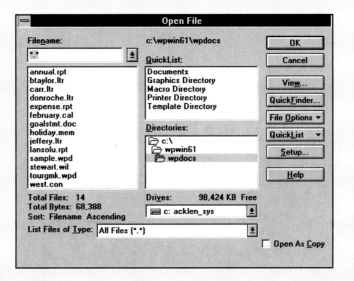

6 Click the Cancel button.

Clicking the Cancel button closes the dialog box without selecting any options or performing any actions. In the next lesson, you learn how to customize WordPerfect.

WordPerfect uses symbols in its menus to let you know what happens when you select the menu item. Many commands need more information from you before the computer can carry out the commands. You give this information either by responding to dialog boxes or by choosing a more specific command.

If you see an ellipsis (...) next to an item, that means a dialog box appears when you select that item. If you see an arrow (▶), that means another menu follows that command. If you don't see anything next to an item (**Ex**it on the **F**ile menu, for example), that command doesn't need any more information from you.

Shortcut keys also appear next to some menu items. These keys give you fast ways to choose WordPerfect commands using the keyboard. For example, the shortcut key for the **O**pen command on the **F**ile menu is [Ctrl]+ [O].

Lesson 4: Customizing WordPerfect

Default
Automatic settings that the computer uses unless you specify other settings.

As you have seen, the *default* WordPerfect screen contains a Toolbar, Power Bar, and Status Bar to help you quickly accomplish common tasks in WordPerfect. If you prefer, you can turn these elements off so they don't display on-screen, which gives you more room on your screen for text. WordPerfect also has a Ruler Bar (which is not shown on the default WordPerfect screen) that you can turn on and use to set tabs and margins quickly.

You can also customize many areas of the program to suit your unique work habits by using the Preferences dialog box. When you modify these settings, the changes take effect immediately and remain in effect until you change them again.

In this lesson, you learn how to turn on and off the displays of the Power Bar, Toolbar and Ruler Bar as well as how to get to the Preferences dialog box.

To Customize WordPerfect

❶ Choose View from the menu bar.

The **V**iew menu has options for the Toolbar, Power Bar, the Ruler Bar, and the Status Bar (see Figure 1.6). A check mark appears next to the menu command when the screen element is turned on. Notice the check marks next to the Toolbar, Power Bar, and Status Bar, which are turned on by default.

Figure 1.6
The **V**iew menu commands let you customize the WordPerfect window.

Check mark ———————→

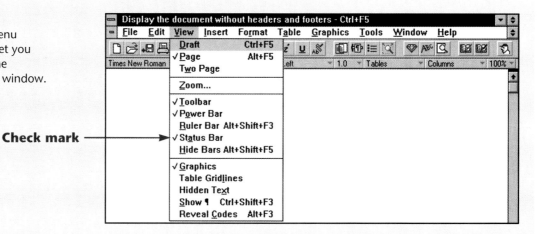

❷ Choose Power Bar from the View menu.

Because the Power Bar is turned on by default, when you choose the Power Bar, your action *deselects* the option and turns the Power Bar off. Look at the top of the screen, and notice that you can no longer see the Power Bar.

continues

The Short, Happy Life of the Wang

What does the word Wang mean to you? During the late 70s and early 80s, the term *Wang* became synonymous with word processing. At that time, Wang word processing systems were the undisputed leaders in the word processing market, and although its success was short-lived, Wang contributed many of the features used in word processing software today.

Wang was founded by Dr. An Wang, a brilliant Chinese immigrant who built a corporate giant from scratch. Wang introduced the first CRT-based word processing system in 1976, and within two years of its development, Wang became the largest worldwide supplier of such systems. Wang word processing systems consisted of a central processing unit that served several terminals dedicated only to the task of word processing the Wang way.

During the 1970s, Wang Labs grew at an annual rate of 67 percent. The value of Wang stock skyrocketed from $6 a share in 1976 to $800 a share in 1983! By 1985, Wang had developed into a worldwide giant with over 30,000 employees and revenues of $3 billion. The people of Wang began to think anything was possible under the guidance of their enigmatic founder, universally known as the Doctor. By 1989, however, Wang sustained a stunning $424 million loss for the fiscal year. In only four years, the company's stock had lost more than 90 percent of its value, during the greatest boom market in history.

What happened to Wang? Even during Wang's heyday, warning signs indicated trouble ahead. The company had borrowed and expanded with unrestrained optimism. The twelve-story corporate headquarters had lavish decorations, and top management traveled in a $14 million corporate jet that even included china bearing the Wang logo.

The days of dedicated word processing were numbered by 1981, when IBM introduced its Personal Computer. At first, word processing software for microcomputers didn't have all the features available on the Wang. Soon, however, products such as WordPerfect, WordStar, and Multimate boasted of powerful word processing capabilities.

At first, Wang's customers were slow to abandon their sizable investment in Wang equipment. Law firms stayed especially loyal to Wang because many of the lawyers didn't want to have computers on their desks. Yet, companies soon realized that PCs offered more power and flexibility than a machine like the Wang, which was dedicated to one specific task.

Wang was a multibillion-dollar company, but it was slow to adapt to the new PC world. The personal computer rapidly replaced the Wang, as the company watched its market leadership slip away. Nonetheless, Wang word processing will always be remembered for its contribution to PC software such as Word and WordPerfect that is used today.

For further information relating to this topic, see Unit 4A, "Word Processing and Desktop Publishing," of **Computers In Your Future** *by Marilyn Meyer and Roberta Baber.*

To Customize WordPerfect   (continued)

❸ From the menu bar, choose View.

Toggle switch

A single menu command used to turn a feature both on and off. If the feature is already on, selecting the menu command turns it off, and vice versa.

Now that you have turned the Power Bar off, the check mark no longer appears next to the menu command. The commands to display the Toolbar, Power Bar, Ruler Bar, and Status Bar are *toggle switches*. If the element is already displayed, selecting the menu command turns the command off; if the element is not displayed, selecting the menu command turns the command on.

❹ Choose Power Bar.

The Power Bar reappears on-screen below the Toolbar. In the next step, you turn on the display of the **R**uler Bar.

❺ Choose View; then choose Ruler Bar.

The Ruler Bar appears on-screen, below the Power Bar (see Figure 1.7). You use the Ruler Bar to quickly change the tab settings and the left and right margins for the current document. Because you won't use the Ruler Bar as frequently as the Toolbar or the Power Bar and it takes up space, turn the Ruler Bar back off now.

Figure 1.7
The **R**uler Bar displays the current tab and left/right margin settings.

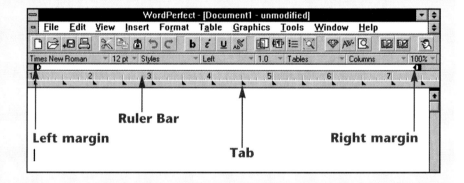

❻ Choose View from the menu bar; then choose Ruler Bar.

You just turned off the Ruler Bar. The Toolbar, which displays underneath the menu bar, is one of 15 different Toolbars that come with the program. WordPerfect has Toolbars for working with fonts, graphics, tables, legal documents, macros, and so forth. Display the list of Toolbars now.

❼ Move the mouse pointer to any icon on the Toolbar, and click the right mouse button.

The right mouse button displays a QuickMenu for the Toolbar, which lists the available Toolbars with options to edit, set preferences for, and hide the Toolbar (see Figure 1.8). Notice the check mark next to the 6.1 WordPerfect Toolbar—the default Toolbar. To select another Toolbar, move the mouse pointer to the Toolbar name, and click the left mouse button.

Figure 1.8
The Toolbar QuickMenu lists the available toolbars.

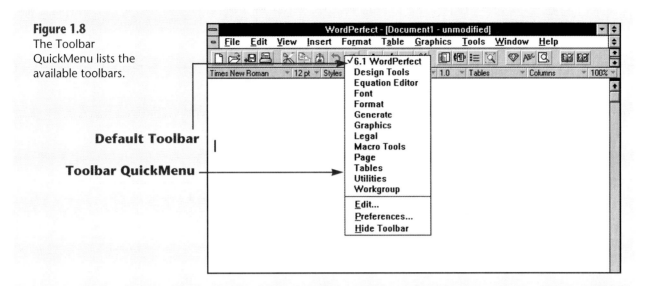

Default Toolbar

Toolbar QuickMenu

If you have problems...

Make sure you click the *right* mouse button to display the list of Toolbars. If you accidentally click the *left* mouse button on the Toolbar, you click the icon where the mouse pointer is resting. Cancel the menu or dialog box (if one appears), and try again.

❽ Move the mouse pointer to the document window, and click the left mouse button.

Clicking inside the document window clears the Toolbar QuickMenu. Finally, take a look at the Preferences dialog box to get an idea of the different areas of the program that you can customize.

❾ From the menu bar, choose Edit.

This action opens the **E**dit menu, which lists the WordPerfect editing commands. The Pr**e**ferences menu command appears at the bottom of the **E**dit menu.

❿ Choose Preferences.

The Preferences dialog box appears, and lists the 12 different areas of the program that you can customize (see Figure 1.9). Your changes take effect immediately, so they affect the current document and any new documents that you create.

continues

To Customize WordPerfect (continued)

Figure 1.9
Use the options in the Preferences dialog box to customize different areas of the Word-Perfect program.

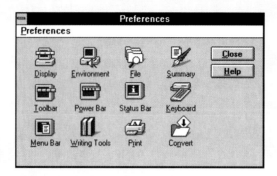

⑪ Choose Close.

The Close option shuts the dialog box. If you have made any changes, they are saved when you close the dialog box. In the next lesson, you learn to use the Help system.

Jargon Watch

QuickMenus appear when you right-click in various parts of the program. For example, you can right-click inside the document window to display a QuickMenu of the editing commands. If you right-click inside a file list (in the Open File dialog box, for example), you get a QuickMenu with file management commands.

Lesson 5: Getting Help

By now, you probably realize that you may run into problems as you work with your computer and with software such as WordPerfect for Windows. If you find you need a quick solution to a problem with WordPerfect, you can use the Help system, a feature of the software. The Help system makes it easy to search for information on the topic that interests you. WordPerfect Help also provides coaches and tutorials to teach you the basics of WordPerfect.

In this lesson, you use the Search feature of Help to find more information about margins. Try using WordPerfect Help now.

To Get Help

❶ Choose Help from the menu bar.

The **H**elp menu displays a number of options available to you when you use Help. Table 1.2 (on page 17) lists the items on the **H**elp menu and gives you a brief description of each one.

❷ Choose Search for Help On.

The Search dialog box appears (see Figure 1.10). The Search dialog box helps you find information on a specific topic.

Figure 1.10
Use the Search dialog
box to search for help
topics by a keyword.

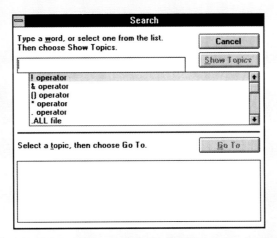

❸ In the text box, type margins.

As you type the keyword margins, WordPerfect scrolls through the
list of Help topics until it finds a match. Now, display a list of Help
topics that relate to the keyword.

❹ Choose Show Topics.

WordPerfect displays a list of related Help topics in the first list box.

❺ Choose Margins from the second list box (see Figure 1.11).

Figure 1.11
Choose a more detailed
topic from the second
list box.

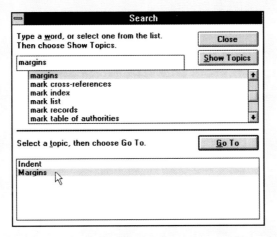

❻ Click the Go To button.

The Help screen appears with detailed information about margins
(see Figure 1.12). Note that the mouse pointer changes to a pointing
hand when you position it over a Help item that leads to more
information. For example, if you point to an underlined word or
phrase, the mouse changes to a hand. You can then click that word
or phrase to reveal more information.

continues

Figure 1.12
The Help window offers information about margins.

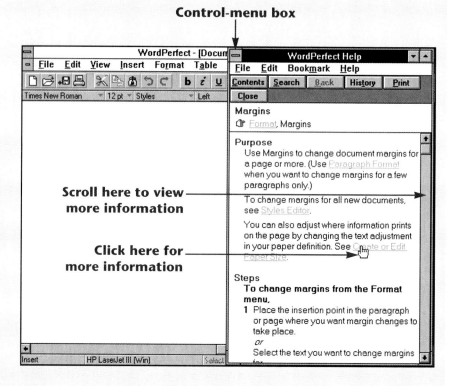

Control-menu box

Scroll here to view more information

Click here for more information

⑦ Double-click the Control-menu box.

This action closes Help and returns you to WordPerfect. You learn how to exit WordPerfect in the next lesson.

You can use several keyboard shortcuts to get Help. If you are in a menu, you can press F1 to display the Help screen for that menu. If you are in the document window, pressing F1 will display the Help Contents screen. This is sometimes called *context-sensitive* help. If you press Shift + F1, the mouse pointer turns into an arrow with a question mark. Click any part of the screen with this pointer to identify the feature and bring up the appropriate Help screen.

Jargon Watch

WordPerfect provides what's called **on-line, context-sensitive** help. Sounds pretty complicated, doesn't it? Well, this form of help is actually very easy to use.

When you hear that something is **on-line**, that means that it's hooked up to your computer. In this case, the term lets you know that you can get help through your computer, as opposed to a book or an instructor.

Context-sensitive help means that you can get help about the specific topic you are using at the moment. In other words, if you are in the Open File dialog box, you can get help about managing files simply by pressing F1.

Table 1.2 The Help Menu	
Item	Function
Contents	Displays the Help Contents screen, which contains the How Do I, Examples, Search, Additional Help, Macros and Using Help topics.
Search for Help on	Opens the Search dialog box, which lets you search for a particular Help topic.
How Do I	Displays a list of common tasks for which you can get step-by-step instructions.
Macros	Displays help on WordPerfect's Macro Language.
C**o**aches	Displays a list of automated procedures that help you learn a task.
Upgrade Expert	Helps you move from a previous version of WordPerfect, Word for Windows, or Ami Pro to WordPerfect.
Tutorial	Runs the WordPerfect Tutorial program, which teaches you the basics of WordPerfect.
About WordPerfect	Displays WordPerfect program release and system resource information.

Lesson 6: Exiting WordPerfect

When you finish working, you should exit WordPerfect and Windows before you turn off your computer. You avoid losing any of your work by getting into this habit. If you turn off the computer before exiting the program, you may lose some of your data. Complete this project by closing your file and exiting the WordPerfect and Windows software.

To Exit WordPerfect

❶ Open the File menu, and choose Exit.

If you experimented by typing text into the document window, WordPerfect displays a message box that asks if you want to save changes to DOCUMENT1 (see Figure 1.13).

Figure 1.13
This message box may save changes in DOCUMENT1.

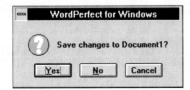

continues

To Exit WordPerfect　(continued)

Because you were just practicing, you don't need to save the changes. Choose **N**o to exit the program without saving the changes. If you didn't enter any text, the program simply closes.

Once you have closed WordPerfect, the Windows Program Manager appears, as long as no other software applications are running.

If you have completed your session on the computer, proceed with step 2. Otherwise, continue with the "Applying Your Skills" case studies at the end of this project.

2 To exit Windows, open the File menu, and choose the Exit Windows command.

Windows displays a confirmation message box.

3 Choose OK.

Windows closes and returns you to the DOS prompt. When the DOS prompt appears, you can safely turn off the computer.

You can double-click the Control-menu box to exit any file or program you are currently using. For example, double-clicking the document Control-menu box (next to the menu bar of a document) closes the document. Double-clicking the Control-menu box in the WordPerfect title bar exits WordPerfect, and double-clicking the application Control-menu box in the Windows title bar exits Windows. Again, you are prompted to save any unsaved work before you close any file or application.

If you prefer to use the keyboard, you can use Alt + F4 , the keyboard shortcut noted next to the **F**ile, **E**xit command.

Checking Your Skills

True/False

For each of the following statements, check *T* or *F* to indicate whether the statement is true or false.

__T __F　**1.** To open a menu from the menu bar, you move the mouse pointer to the menu name, and click the right mouse button.

__T __F　**2.** You can cancel a dialog box without making any changes by clicking the Cancel button.

__T __F　**3.** The Power Bar is used to quickly change the tab settings and the left and right margins.

__T __F　**4.** You can double-click the document Control-menu box to exit WordPerfect for Windows.

__T __F　**5.** The Toolbar contains all the menu names to access the menu commands.

Multiple Choice

Circle the letter of the correct answer for each of the following.

1. The term DOS stands for _____.

   a. Drive Operating System

   b. Disk Operating System

   c. Disk Operational Services

   d. none of the above

2. The correct command you type at the DOS prompt to start Windows is _____.

   a. **window**

   b. **windows**

   c. **win**

   d. **run windows**

3. Which of the following screen components does WordPerfect have?

   a. button pad

   b. menu list

   c. toolbar

   d. status line

4. A(n) _____ next to a menu command indicates a dialog box appears when that item is selected.

   a. arrow pointing to the left

   b. ellipsis

   c. small filled circle

   d. asterisk

5. The **F**ile menu contains which of the following menu items?

   a. **O**pen

   b. **S**end

   c. Document Information

   d. all the above

Completion

In the blank provided, write the correct answer for each of the following statements.

1. To open a menu with the keyboard, you press the _____ key plus the underlined letter.

2. Press _____ to display the **H**elp **C**ontents screen.

3. The WordPerfect _____ feature teaches you how to perform common tasks by prompting you through each step.

4. You can use the _____ dialog box to look for help topics that contain a keyword.

5. The Minimize/Maximize buttons on the _____ control the current document.

Screen ID

Label each element of the WordPerfect for Windows screen shown in Figure 1.14.

1. _____

2. _____

3. _____

4. _____

5. _____

6. _____

7. _____

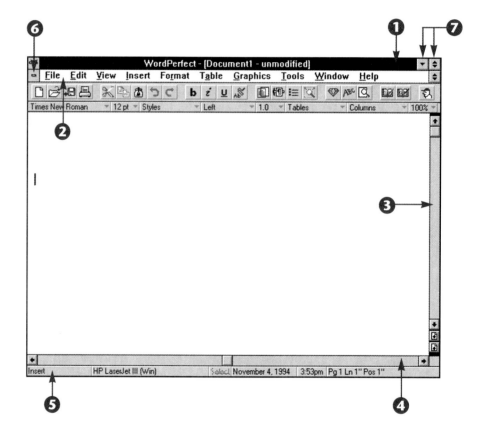

Applying Your Skills

At the end of each project in *WordPerfect for Windows Essentials,* you can learn how to apply your WordPerfect skills to various personal and business situations. "On Your Own" case studies let you try using the skills you just learned to create WordPerfect applications you can use at home or at school. You can use the "Brief Cases" case study to learn about how WordPerfect can be used in managing a business.

Take a few minutes to work through these case studies now.

On Your Own

Learning about Menus

Now that you have been introduced to the WordPerfect screen and WordPerfect's Help system, use these skills to continue to explore the program. For this case study, you open several more menus to get a better idea of what features WordPerfect has available and how they are organized. You also use the Examples section to see samples of documents that you can create in WordPerfect.

To Learn More about Menus

1. From the menu bar, choose **E**dit.

2. Next, choose **V**iew from the menu bar.

3. Now open the **I**nsert menu.

4. Continue opening each menu until you have opened all the menus on the menu bar.

5. Open the Fo**r**mat menu.

6. Drag the mouse pointer down to move through the Fo**r**mat menu items. Use the mouse pointer to open and close the submenus for **L**ine, **P**aragraph, **P**age, **D**ocument, **C**olumns, **J**ustification and **T**ypesetting.

7. Cancel the menus without making any changes.

To View Sample Documents

1. Choose **H**elp from the menu bar.

2. Choose **C**ontents from the **H**elp menu.

3. Choose Examples from the **C**ontents screen.

4. Click a sample document from the left side of the Indexes dialog box to see a brief description of the document and the features used to create the document.

5. Click a red arrow, located on the right side of the sample document in the Indexes dialog box, to display a Help screen on that particular element.

6. When you finish, choose **C**lose from the Indexes dialog box; then choose **F**ile, E**x**it from the Help dialog box.

Brief Cases

Planning Documents

"Brief Cases" case studies help you learn how business managers and staff use WordPerfect for Windows. As you work through this continuing case study, you learn how to set up and run your own business with the help of software such as WordPerfect.

If you have already used other books in the Que College *Essentials* series, you have learned how other software applications can help a small, start-up business such as Sound Byte Music, our example in the "Brief Cases" case study. If you haven't used other *Essentials* books before, imagine that you are the owner and hands-on business manager of Sound Byte Music, a new music store located in a college town.

For this case study, think about the kinds of documents you need to create in WordPerfect to help you run Sound Byte Music. Make a list of all the types of documents you think you will use. Consider all the things you need to communicate in writing to keep your business running smoothly. Note which features of WordPerfect you think will make creating each kind of document easier.

Creating New Documents

Creating a Cover Letter for Your Resume

In this project, you learn how to

- ➤ Enter Text into a Document
- ➤ Save a Document
- ➤ Open an Existing Document
- ➤ Move around in a Document
- ➤ Correct Text
- ➤ Insert New Text
- ➤ Print a Document

Why Would I Do This?

ow that you have become familiar with the WordPerfect for Windows screen and the benefits of using word processing software, it's time to put WordPerfect to work for you. One of the most common uses for word processing software is to create simple documents, such as letters and memos. In this project, you learn how to create a cover letter for your own resume—one of the most useful letters you can write.

Using the sample information and instructions provided in this project, you work through the steps it takes to enter text and create a document. You can then make necessary corrections, save changes, and print the final result.

Lesson 1: Entering Text into a Document

You can begin entering text for your cover letter as soon as you start WordPerfect for Windows because a new document, titled DOCUMENT1, automatically appears on-screen. For your convenience, DOCUMENT1 provides basic settings for margins, tabs, type style, type size, and paper size. This formatting set-up is defined in the default document template called STANDARD.WPT.

For your cover letter, use the document format WordPerfect provides and start entering sample text using the steps that follow.

To Enter Text into a Document

1 Using the steps in Project 1, start Windows and WordPerfect for Windows.

WordPerfect starts with a new document titled DOCUMENT1. The insertion point appears as a blinking vertical bar at the upper left corner of the document window. You type the text for your letter at the insertion point.

2 Type the following text:

> **Your advertisement in The Indianapolis Star for a new marketing associate is of great interest to me. As a recent graduate of the Indiana University School of Business, my degree in marketing gives me many of the skills you seek. I also have a minor in Spanish—perfect for working with your international accounts.**

Don't stop or press ⏎Enter when you reach the end of a line. WordPerfect automatically moves, or *wraps*, any text that won't fit on the current line down to the line that follows.

❸ Press ⏎Enter **twice when you reach the end of the paragraph you have been asked to type.**

Pressing ⏎Enter tells WordPerfect to go to the next line. By pressing ⏎Enter twice, you tell WordPerfect to end the paragraph and then create a blank line between the first and second paragraphs.

❹ Choose View, and then choose Show ¶.

Choosing **V**iew, **S**how ¶ displays the hard returns you just entered. When you turn on the **S**how feature, WordPerfect shows non-printing characters such as hard returns, spaces, and tabs. Notice the paragraph symbol that appears where you pressed ⏎Enter. Viewing the document this way makes it easy to see where you pressed the **spacebar** and ⏎Enter.

❺ Type the following text:

> **I believe that that I can be very successful in the fast-paced work environment that you describe, but the only way to find out is to talk with me in person. Please review the enclosed resume and call me at 555-3912 to schedule an interview. I am available to meet on Tuesday and Thursday afternoons.**

❻ Press ⏎Enter **at the end of the paragraph.**

Notice that WordPerfect inserted a paragraph symbol to show the hard return you typed. Make sure you type the double that in the first line—you delete the extra that in a later section. After you have finished entering the sample text, check to see how closely your screen matches Figure 2.1.

Figure 2.1
The draft cover letter in a new document window.

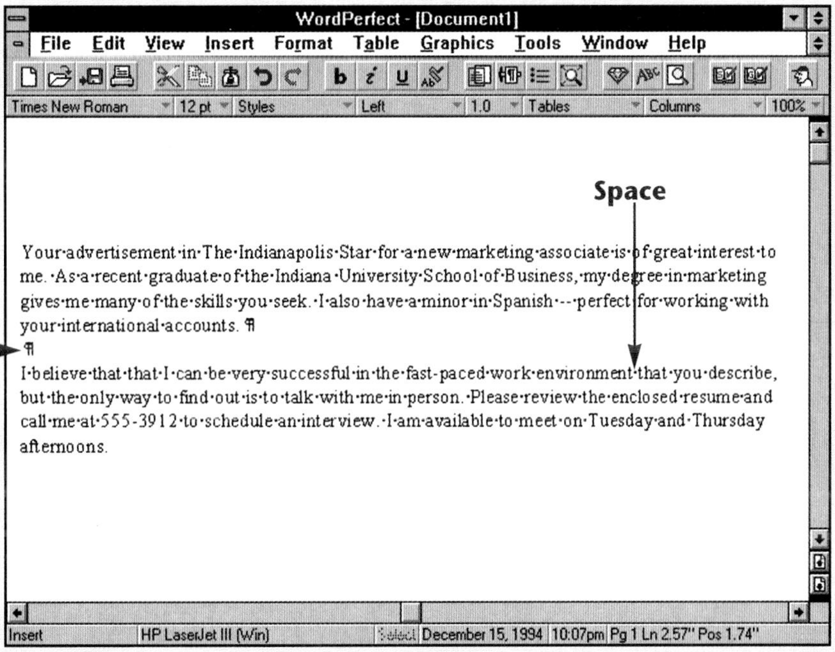

Hard return

continues

To Enter Text into a Document (continued)

7 Choose View, and then choose Show ¶ again.

Because you have finished entering text for now, you can hide the non-printing characters. It's wise to save your work from time to time, especially when you have just entered a lot of text. You learn how to save your work in Lesson 2. For now, leave the document open. You continue to work with the cover letter you created throughout this project.

Jargon Watch

When you hear people talk about **hard returns**, they may also mention something called a **soft return**. Soft returns occur at the end of every line you type where text is automatically **wrapped**, or moved down to the next line. Hard returns are inserted where you want a paragraph to end or where you want a short line. You insert a hard return by pressing ⏎Enter.

The document **template** discussed at the beginning of this section is simply a set of stored format settings that you can use each time you create a document. If you want every document you write to look like the one you just created, you can continue to use the default template, STANDARD.WPT. WordPerfect provides a wide variety of templates for you to use in creating other documents in your work.

While you type, you may make mistakes that you notice immediately and want to correct. You can use ⬅Backspace or Del to remove one character at a time. When you press ⬅Backspace, you delete the character immediately to the left of the insertion point. The Del key erases the character immediately to the right of the insertion point.

To delete an entire word, position the insertion point anywhere in the word, and select the word by double-clicking it with the mouse. After you have selected the word, you can make it disappear by pressing Del.

Lesson 2: Saving a Document

At this point, you have not safely stored any of the text you entered in your cover letter for future use. At the moment, your letter is stored in the computer's *random access memory*, or *RAM*. If your computer *crashed*, you would lose all the work you just finished. For this reason, you should save your work every 5-10 minutes. You can save your work to the *hard disk* (also called the *hard drive*) inside the computer or to a *floppy disk* that you can take with you.

So that you don't lose any of your valuable work (or your valuable time), save your cover letter now.

To Save a Document

❶ From the menu bar, choose File.

Choosing **F**ile opens the **F**ile menu (see Figure 2.2).

Figure 2.2
The **F**ile menu.

Click here to save
the document

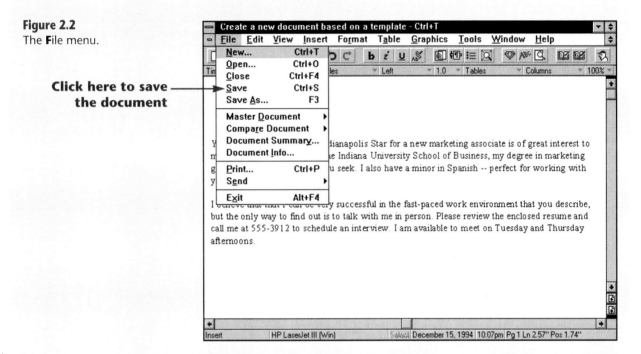

❷ Choose Save to display the Save As dialog box.

If you haven't yet saved and named the document, choosing either **S**ave or Save **A**s will open the Save As dialog box (see Figure 2.3). Now type a name for your letter in the File**n**ame text box. You can type a name of up to eight characters, including letters, numbers, and symbols, but you can't use spaces in your file name.

Figure 2.3
The Save As dialog box.

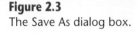

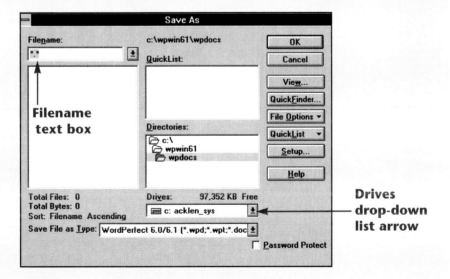

Drives
drop-down
list arrow

continues

To Save a Document   (continued)

❸ Type coverltr in the Filename text box.

You can type file names in upper case, lower case, or both—WordPerfect automatically converts the names to lower case.

❹ Click the Drives drop-down list arrow; then click the drive where you want to save your letter.

In the Save As dialog box, WordPerfect automatically proposes to save the letter in the default directory on the default drive. If you want to save to a different drive, perhaps a floppy disk, choose the drive from the list as shown in Figure 2.4. If you want, you can also select a different directory from the **D**irectories list.

Figure 2.4
The Save As dialog box with the Drives list open.

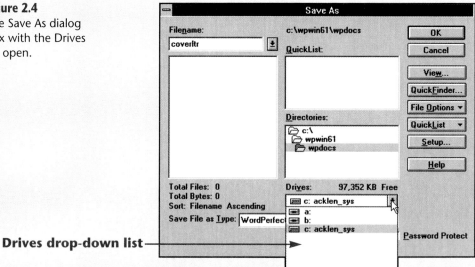

Drives drop-down list

If you have problems...

If you try to save to a floppy disk and you get an error message, check two things. First, be sure you have selected the correct drive. Many computers have more than one floppy drive. Try selecting another drive and see if that fixes the problem.

Second, be sure you use a formatted disk. If you try to use an unformatted disk, you should see an error message that tells you the disk you selected is not formatted. The error message may ask if you want to format the disk now. If you want to format the disk so you can save files to it, choose **Y**es; then follow the instructions until the disk formatting is complete.

Be very careful when formatting disks—and don't format a hard disk drive. When you format a disk, you erase all information stored on the disk. If you have any questions about formatting or disk drives, don't hesitate to ask your instructor.

⑤ Choose OK.

This action saves a copy of your letter as a file called COVERLTR.WPD. WordPerfect automatically adds the three-letter file extension WPD for whatever name you type—you don't need to type the extension. However, if you want to use another extension, you can type it with the file name. The Save As dialog box closes, and the new file name, COVERLTR.WPD, appears in the document window title bar.

⑥ Click the Save icon.

This action shows you the quickest way to save a document as you work. After you save a document for the first time, you can save the document again with the same name, and to the same drive and directory, by clicking the Save icon on the Toolbar. If you want to save an existing document with a different name or to a different drive or directory, choose Save **A**s from the **F**ile menu.

⑦ Choose File, and then choose Close.

This action closes the COVERLTR.WPD document. In the next lesson, you open this document (an existing document) again so that you can complete the letter.

Jargon Watch

Once again, you have faced a lot of computer jargon in this lesson. When people start referring to how much **RAM** their computer has, don't let it throw you. RAM stands for **random-access memory**, the temporary storage space the computer uses for programs it is working with at present.

When a computer **crashes**, it just means some kind of error—either with the **software** (a program the computer is running), or in the **hardware** (for example, the power supply or hard drive)—has caused the computer to stop working. Everything stored in RAM is lost when a crash occurs.

Again, that is why you need to save your work frequently to a **hard disk** or a **floppy disk**. Floppy disks are the small disks you can carry around with you from computer to computer, providing a back-up copy of important information. Even though the 3 1/2 inch variety of floppy disk has a hard outer case, the disk inside is indeed flexible. Hard disks (or hard drives), the hard platters inside your computer, look very similar to the CDs you buy in a music store. Your computer stores the bulk of the programs and data it uses on the hard disk.

Lesson 3: Opening an Existing Document

Now that you have created a cover letter by typing in the basic information, you may want to make some corrections or changes. Before you make any changes or add new text, you need to open the document again.

When you open an existing document, WordPerfect opens a new document window and displays the document you need. Throughout this book, you open existing documents supplied to your instructor, which you then save using a more realistic file name. Saving a document under a different name lets you use the original, unchanged document at a later time.

Now try opening the cover letter you created in the preceding lesson.

To Open an Existing Document

❶ Click the Open icon on the Toolbar.

WordPerfect displays the Open File dialog box (see Figure 2.5). You can also access this dialog box by choosing **O**pen from the **F**ile menu.

❷ Choose the appropriate drive and directory.

Check to see if the COVERLTR.WPD file appears in the File**n**ame text box (see Figure 2.5). You may have to scroll through the list to find the file. If you don't find the file, it is probably on another drive or in another directory. Make sure you look at the correct drive and directory.

Figure 2.5
The Open dialog box.

Click here to select the cover letter file →

← Click here to open the cover letter

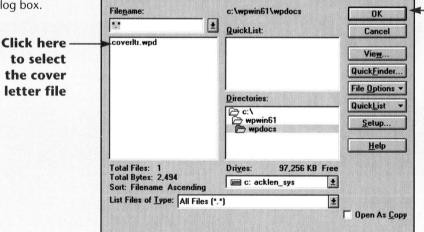

❸ Click COVERLTR.WPD in the Filename list.

The file name COVERLTR.WPD appears in the File**n**ame text box.

❹ Choose OK.

WordPerfect places the cover letter in a new document window with the file name COVERLTR.WPD displayed in the title bar (see Figure 2.6). You can now begin working again on your cover letter. Keep COVERLTR.**WPD** open because you continue to work with it for the rest of this project.

Figure 2.6
Your cover letter open
in a document window.

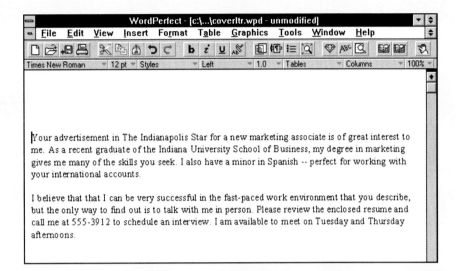

 In the Open File dialog box, instead of selecting the name of the document and choosing OK, you have another option. To open the file, you can simply double-click the name of the document you want to open in the Filename list box. You can use this technique with most dialog boxes.

Lesson 4: Moving around in a Document

To make changes and corrections quickly and easily, you need to learn the various ways of moving around in a document. For example, you can use either the mouse or the keyboard to move the insertion point in WordPerfect. Table 2.1 on page (xx) shows useful keyboard shortcuts for moving around a document.

Your cover letter, COVERLTR.WPD, should be open and ready for work. Practice moving around in the cover letter using both the mouse and keyboard now.

To Move around in a Document

❶ **In COVERLTR.WPD, press** Ctrl + End.

This action moves the insertion point to the end of the document (see Figure 2.7).

continues

To Move around in a Document (continued)

Figure 2.7
The cover letter with the insertion point at the end of the document.

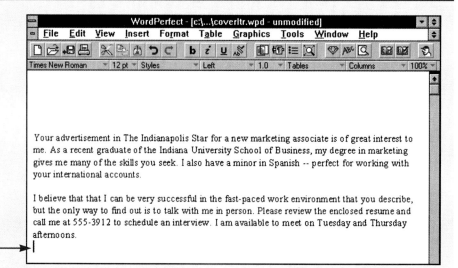

Insertion point ──────▶

Your advertisement in The Indianapolis Star for a new marketing associate is of great interest to me. As a recent graduate of the Indiana University School of Business, my degree in marketing gives me many of the skills you seek. I also have a minor in Spanish -- perfect for working with your international accounts.

I believe that that I can be very successful in the fast-paced work environment that you describe, but the only way to find out is to talk with me in person. Please review the enclosed resume and call me at 555-3912 to schedule an interview. I am available to meet on Tuesday and Thursday afternoons.

❷ Position the mouse pointer between the 1 and the 2 in the phone number 555-3912; then click the left mouse button.

Clicking the mouse while the mouse pointer is shaped like a vertical bar moves the insertion point to the location you select. Any new text that you enter or any changes that you make will happen here.

❸ On the vertical scroll bar, click the area between the scroll box and the bottom arrow.

This action scrolls the document down one screen at a time to the end of the document—you can scroll up or down this way. You may be surprised to see that you have a virtually blank document window. Don't panic—you have simply moved to the very end of the document (see Figure 2.8). Keep in mind, however, that the insertion point has not moved. The insertion point remains in the phone number, where you last positioned it.

Figure 2.8
The bold line indicates
the bottom edge of
the page.

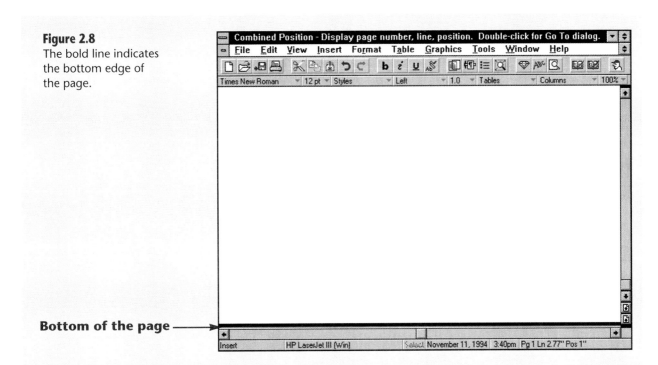

Bottom of the page ⟶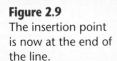

④ Drag the scroll box to the top of the scroll bar.

This action scrolls the document back into view. Now, practice
moving the insertion point with the keyboard.

⑤ Press ↑ two times.

The insertion point moves to the first line in the second paragraph.

⑥ Press End.

The insertion point moves to the end of the line. Compare your
cover letter with the screen in Figure 2.9. Your screen should now
look like this figure.

Figure 2.9
The insertion point
is now at the end of
the line.

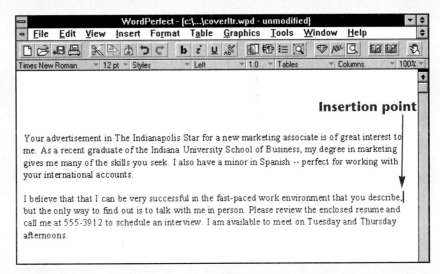

continues

To Move around in a Document (continued)

❼ Move the insertion point to the beginning of the document using whichever method you prefer.
In most cases, you save your changes to the document before continuing to the next lesson. Because you just practiced moving around in the document (and you made no changes) in this lesson, you don't need to save the document now. In the next lesson, you learn how to correct your text.

Table 2.1 Keyboard Shortcuts for Moving around in a Document

Key	Action
←	Moves the insertion point one character to the left.
→	Moves the insertion point one character to the right.
↑	Moves the insertion point up one line.
↓	Moves the insertion point down one line.
Home	Moves the insertion point to the beginning of the line.
End	Moves the insertion point to the end of the line.
PgUp	Moves the insertion point up by the height of one window.
PgDn	Moves the insertion point down by the height of one window.
Ctrl+ Home	Moves the insertion point to the beginning of the document.
Ctrl+ End	Moves the insertion point to the end of the document.

You can go directly to a specific location using the Go To dialog box. The quickest way to open the Go To dialog box is to press Ctrl+ G. If you want to use the mouse to open the Go To dialog box, double-click the position area of the status line (where the current page number, line, and position are indicated).

Once you are in the Go To dialog box, you can move to a specific page, bookmark, table, or other part of the document using options in the Go To dialog box. Choose OK when you have made your selection, or choose Cancel if you change your mind.

Lesson 5: Correcting Text

After you read the first draft of your letter, you may decide that you don't like the way a particular sentence sounds, or you may find that you have simply entered the wrong information. WordPerfect allows you to delete text you don't want, enter new text, and correct existing text.

You can save a lot of time and effort by changing existing documents and saving them as new versions. For example, once you create a cover letter, like the one for the marketing position in this example, you can change the letter and use it again as a cover letter for a different job opening.

Try correcting text now using the steps in this lesson.

To Correct Text

❶ In COVERLTR.WPD, double-click the word perfect in the third line of the first paragraph.

The word perfect appears selected (see Figure 2.10).

❷ Press Del.

You erased the word **perfect**.

Figure 2.10
The word perfect appears selected.

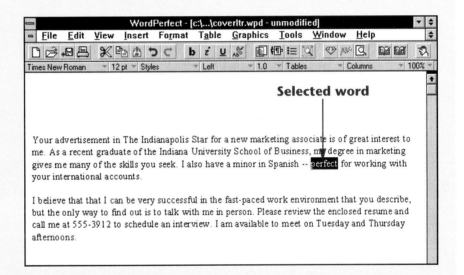

❸ Insert a space; then type ideal to make a slight change in the meaning of this sentence.

Don't forget to type a space before the word *ideal*. Notice that the existing text moves to the right to make room for the new text you just entered, indicating that WordPerfect is in *Insert mode*. Insert mode allows you to enter new text without that text replacing the existing text.

❹ Position the insertion point after the first that in the first line of the second paragraph.

This sentence has a duplicate word—**that**. Delete the first **that** now.

❺ Press ◆Backspace five times to erase the extra that.

Pressing ◆Backspace five times erases the word and the extra space after the word.

❻ Press Ins.

continues

To Correct Text (continued)

Notice that the word *Typeover* appears in the far left corner of the status bar (at the bottom of the document). You have now switched to Typeover mode. When you make a correction in this mode, WordPerfect erases existing text as you type in new text.

7 Position the insertion point before the number 3 in the phone number, which appears near the end of the letter.

8 Type 2193 to insert the correct phone number in this example.

Notice that the new number replaces the old number. Be careful not to type over the wrong text when correcting words in Typeover mode. Compare your letter with the letter in Figure 2.11.

Figure 2.11
The corrected
cover letter.

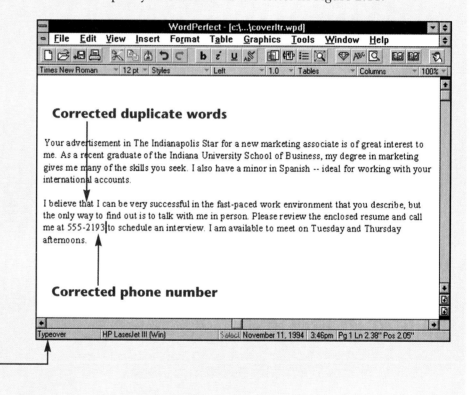

**Typeover
indicator**

9 Press [Ins] again.

This action returns WordPerfect to Insert mode.

10 Click the Save icon on the toolbar.

This action saves the changes you just made to COVERLTR.WPD. Don't close this document because you use it again in the next lesson, where you learn to insert text.

As you just learned, you can switch between **Insert** and **Typeover** mode by pressing [Ins]. The [Ins] key is sometimes called a **toggle key** because it allows you to switch, or "toggle," between two different things. When you start WordPerfect for Windows, WordPerfect uses Insert mode by **default**. A default setting is the way something is automatically done. A **mode** is simply a particular way of doing things.

It may sound impressive to say "WordPerfect for Windows operates in Insert mode by default," but that just means WordPerfect automatically moves text to the right when you type in new text. If you want to type over existing text, just press [Ins].

If you make a mistake as you type or change text, you can use the Undo icon. For example, if you typed over too much text, click on the Undo icon on the Toolbar as many times as you need to go back to your original text. To Redo those same actions, click on the Redo icon in the Toolbar.

WordPerfect also has a way of preventing mistakes. Most people make errors when they type—for example, many people type *adn* when they mean to type *and*, or *hte* instead of *the*. WordPerfect's QuickCorrect feature detects and corrects these and similar types of errors automatically while you type.

If you want to change the QuickCorrect settings, choose the **T**ools menu; then choose **Q**uickCorrect. The QuickCorrect dialog box appears, which lets you add additional words you want corrected (see Figure 2.12). You can also use the QuickCorrect Options dialog box for customizing.

Figure 2.12
The QuickCorrect
dialog box.

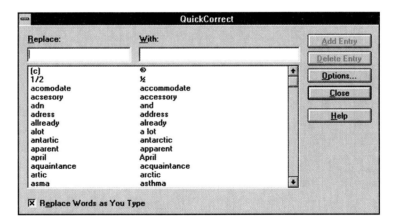

Lesson 6: Inserting New Text

One of the most attractive features of word processing software is the ability to add new information to an existing document. The cover letter you have created is not yet complete. You need to add a mailing address, greeting, and closing to the letter before you can mail it.

Try adding this text now using the following steps.

To Insert New Text

1 **In COVERLTR.WPD, press** Ctrl+Home.

This action moves the insertion point to the beginning of the first paragraph (if it was not already here).

2 **Type June 1, 1995, and press** ↵Enter **twice.**

This action adds the date to your sample letter.

3 **Type the following text:**

> **Ms. Rebecca Keeper**
> **Senior Marketing Manager**
> **Caldwell and Jones**
> **42 Monument Circle**
> **Indianapolis, IN 46260**

Be sure to press ↵Enter at the end of each line you type. Pressing ↵Enter at the end of each of these short lines tells WordPerfect to go to the next line. WordPerfect automatically moves the existing text aside to make room for the new text you enter.

4 **Press** ↵Enter **once again.**

This action tells WordPerfect to leave a blank line after the mailing address. Your letter should look like Figure 2.13.

Figure 2.13
The mailing address added to the letter.

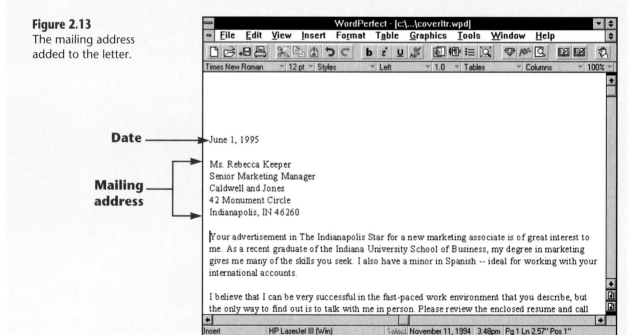

5 **Type the following text:**

> **Dear Ms. Keeper:**

6 **Press** ↵Enter **twice.**

This action tells WordPerfect to go to the next line and leave a blank line between your greeting and the body of your letter.

❼ Press Ctrl+End.

Pressing Ctrl+End moves the insertion point to the end of the document; the insertion point should appear on a blank line below the last line of text in your letter. If you like, you can also use the scroll bar to move to the end of the document. Remember, once you have moved to the end of the document with the scroll bar, you must click inside the document to move the insertion point.

❽ Press ↵Enter.

❾ Type Sincerely, and press ↵Enter **four times.**

This action enters the closing of your letter, leaving enough room for you to sign your name after the word Sincerely. Now compare your letter to the one in Figure 2.14. If you like, you can type your name now to complete the letter.

Figure 2.14
The final cover letter with mailing address, greeting and closing.

Greeting ——————▶

Closing ——————▶

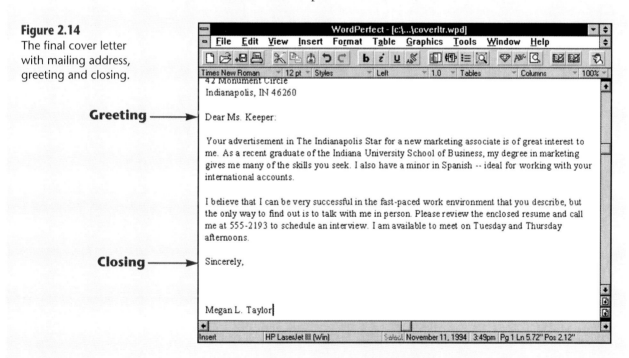

Save your latest changes to COVERLTR.WPD, and keep the file open for the next lesson, where you learn how to print your letter.

Lesson 7: Printing a Document

Now that you have completed your cover letter, you will want to print a paper copy to mail. You may also want to keep an extra paper copy for your files or to review away from the computer. You should save documents immediately before printing them, as you did in Lesson 6.

Try printing the cover letter for your resume now.

To Print a Document

❶ Check the printer.

You can't print if the printer is off, if the printer doesn't have any paper, or if the printer is not *on-line*. Printers often have a light that shows whether the printer is on-line (receiving commands from the computer). You receive an error message if the printer is not on-line.

Once the printer is ready, you need to check the document you are going to print. Use the Zoom feature to display the whole page on your screen.

❷ Click the Zoom button on the Power bar, and choose Full Page.

Choosing this Zoom setting displays your entire page as it will look when printed. Your letter should now look like Figure 2.15. This view of the letter lets you see the text spacing and margins so you have a better idea of how the letter looks on the page. Notice that the letter seems to be squeezed at the top of the page. Add some line spacing to improve the letter's appearance now.

Zoom button

Figure 2.15
Viewing the entire page before printing.

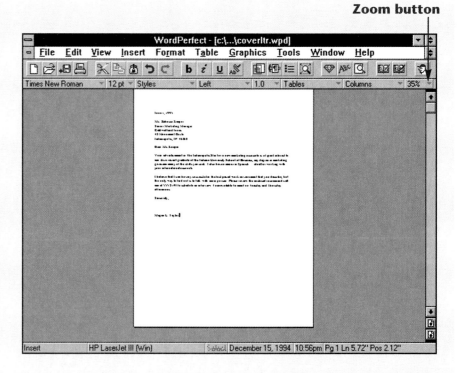

❸ Move the insertion point to the top of the document.

❹ Press ⏎Enter four times.

You have just added more line spacing to the letter so that the letter uses more of the printed page. Do the same thing after the last paragraph.

⑤ Move the insertion point to the blank line between the date and the address; then press ⏎Enter four times.

Compare your letter to the letter in Figure 2.16, and notice the improvement in the spacing on the page.

Figure 2.16
The appearance of the letter improved by additional white space.

Added white space ——

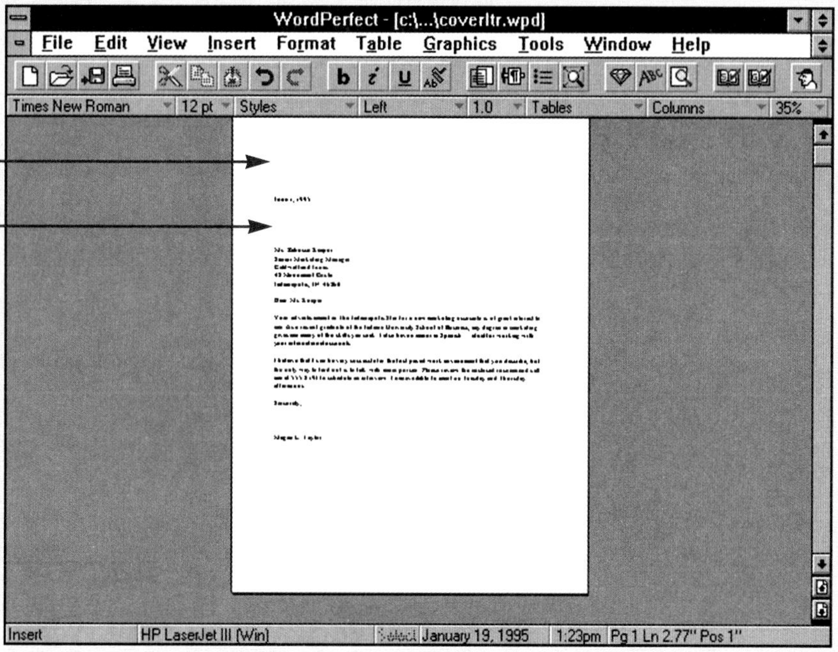

⑥ Click the Zoom button, and choose 100%.

This action changes the Zoom setting back to 100 percent, which takes you back to the setting you were using before you previewed the page. Once you are satisfied with your document's appearance, you can print the document.

⑦ Open the File menu, and choose Print.

This action opens the Print dialog box (see Figure 2.17); you can now choose to print all or part of your document. You can also select another printer, if necessary. By default, WordPerfect prints the full document.

continues

Project 3

Editing Documents

Enhancing Your Resume

In this project, you learn how to

- Select Text
- Enhance Text
- Move and Copy Text
- Use the Undo Feature
- Spell Check a Document
- Use the Thesaurus
- Use the Grammar Checker

Why Would I Do This?

n the last project, you learned how to how to create and edit a document. You learned how to insert and delete text, and how to move around in a document. Now that you know some basic editing techniques, you can learn more about editing in WordPerfect. In this project, you open a sample resume so you can proofread and correct the information. Because your resume is one of the most important documents you can write, the resume needs to look professional, as well as clearly convey your qualifications.

Lesson 1: Selecting Text

After you have typed a document, you may want to go back and make changes to sections of the text. You use the Select feature to define the area of text you want to change. Because you can use either the mouse, the Select menu, or the keyboard to select text, you learn all three techniques in this project. A sample resume has been created for your use in this project, so the first step is to open the file for editing.

If you don't have a copy of the student disk, ask your instructor to tell you which drive and directory contain your student data files. You need these files to work through the lessons in this book.

To Select Text

❶ Open the file PROJ0301.WPD; then save it as RESUME.WPD.

WordPerfect places the resume in a new document window (see Figure 3.1). You can now begin editing the sample resume.

Figure 3.1
The sample resume open in a document window.

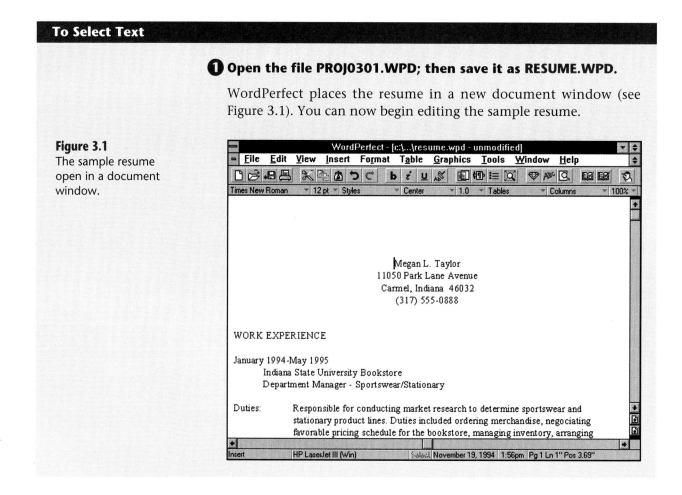

Select
To highlight part of the document so the program knows which information to perform the next action on.

② Move the I-beam mouse pointer to the beginning of the name, located at the top of the resume.

③ Click and drag the mouse down the page.

Selected text appears highlighted (white text on a black background), as shown in Figure 3.2.

Figure 3.2
The resume with selected text.

Selected text ——→

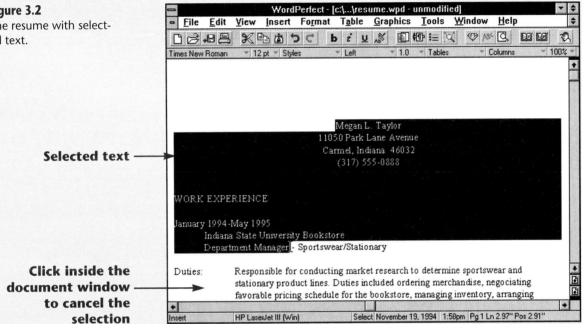

Click inside the document window to cancel the selection ——→

④ As you hold the mouse button down, move the mouse pointer back up through the page.

Performing this action deselects the text. You can use this method if you accidentally select too much text. If you start selecting in the wrong place, you need to cancel the selection and start over.

⑤ Click the mouse pointer inside the document window.

Clicking the mouse pointer inside the document window cancels the current selection.

Clicking and dragging the mouse pointer through the text is the fastest way to select large sections of text. At times, however, you may need to select small sections. Use the mouse shortcuts to select a word and a sentence now.

⑥ Use the vertical scroll bar to scroll down to the Duties description for the University Bookstore.

You don't have to scroll down the page if you already see the first line of the Duties description on your screen.

⑦ Double-click the word sportswear in the first sentence of the Duties description for the University Bookstore (see Figure 3.3).

continues

To Select Text (continued)

Figure 3.3
The sample resume
with a selected word.

**Double-click a
word to select it**

**Triple-click a
sentence to select it**

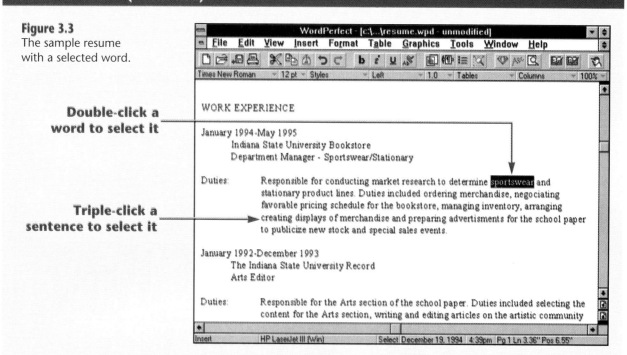

The word sportswear appears highlighted, or selected. Now, select an entire sentence with the mouse.

8 Triple-click the second sentence of the same paragraph.

Triple-clicking a sentence selects the entire sentence; the second sentence should now appear highlighted.

If you have problems...

If the second sentence isn't selected, make sure you click the mouse three times in quick succession, and that you don't move the mouse as you click. If you still have trouble, try using the Select option on the **E**dit menu (explained in the following steps) instead.

9 Click the mouse pointer somewhere in the second sentence.

It doesn't matter where you position the insertion point, as long as it appears *inside* the sentence.

10 Choose Edit, Select.

The Select menu has options to select a sentence, paragraph, a page, or all of the text in a document (see Figure 3.4).

Figure 3.4
The Select menu.

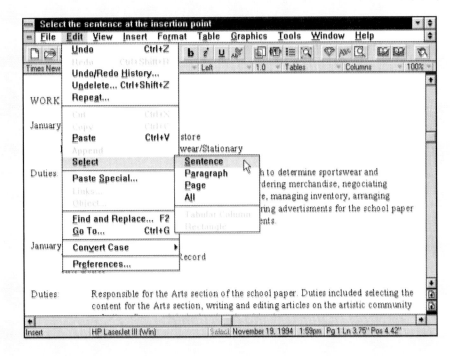

11 **Choose Sentence to select the second sentence of the description.**

The second sentence appears selected.

12 **Click inside the document window to deselect the sentence.**

As you work through the lessons, you want to save the changes you have made to the document in each lesson before going on. In this case, you have just practiced selecting text, so you don't have to save the RESUME.WPD document now. Keep the file open to use in the next lesson.

You can also use the arrow keys on the keyboard to select text. You may find this method more useful when selecting only a small section of text. First, you position the insertion point where you want to start selecting text. Press ⇧Shift); then use the arrow keys to select text. Release ⇧Shift), and press any arrow key to turn the selection off.

You can also use the left margin area to quickly select text. Move the mouse pointer into the left margin area, and notice how the mouse pointer changes to an arrow that points to the right (the normal mouse pointer points to the left). A single click selects the adjacent sentence; a double-click selects the adjacent paragraph.

When selecting sentences, WordPerfect looks for a period to signal the end of a sentence. If you use more than one period in a sentence (*...the amount of $25.15...*), WordPerfect selects the text up to the first period. When selecting paragraphs, WordPerfect looks for a hard return to signal the end of a paragraph. If you have several short lines (like name and address information), each ending in a hard return, WordPerfect treats each line as a paragraph.

Lesson 2: Enhancing Text

Now that you have learned how to select sections of text, try adding some variety and emphasis to the resume by enhancing sections of text with boldface and italics. Each of the headings needs boldface for emphasis and certain elements can be italicized for variety and readability.

To Enhance Text

1 In the file RESUME.WPD, use the "click and drag" method to select the name at the top of the resume-Megan L. Taylor.

Notice that the name and address information is centered between the left and right margins. You learn how to center text in Project 4, "Formatting Documents."

b

2 Click the Bold icon on the Toolbar.

The name now appears in boldface, which makes it stand out from the rest of the text. Click inside the document window to deselect (turn off the selection) so that you can see how the boldface text differs from the regular text (see Figure 3.5).

Figure 3.5
The sample resume with the name in bold.

Click here to bold text

Click here to italicize text

Boldface text

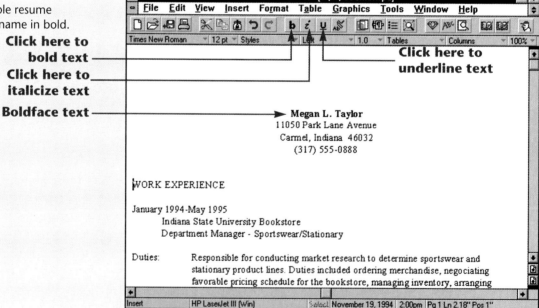

3 Select each of the following headings, and make them bold-face: WORK EXPERIENCE, EDUCATION, **and** REFERENCES AVAILABLE ON REQUEST **phrases.**

b

Each of the major headings should now appear emphasized with boldface text.

4 Select the dates for the first description (January 1994-May 1995).

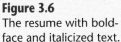 **⑤ Click the Italics icon.**

The use of italicized type in your text adds a more subtle form of emphasis than boldface, and is easier to read than underlining.

⑥ Select the word Duties **next to the first description.**

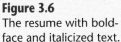 **⑦ Click the Italics icon.**

The Duties heading now appears in italicized type. To make it clear that the word Duties and all the dates are headings, italicize the other two sets.

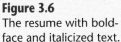 **⑧ Select and italicize the** Duties **heading and the dates for the other two job descriptions.**

Your resume should now look similar to Figure 3.6.

Figure 3.6
The resume with bold-
face and italicized text.

Boldface text ───────▶

Italicized text ───────▶

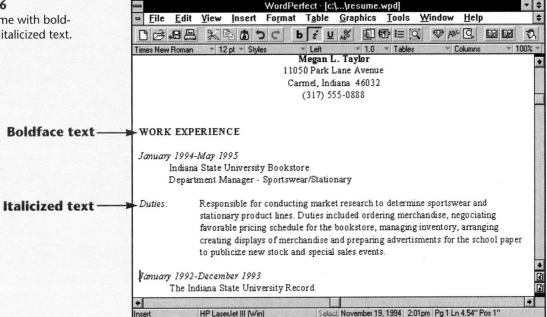

With only minimal effort, you have significantly improved the appearance of a very important document—your resume. Although plain text is neat and easy to read, you want your resume to attract the reader's attention and create a unique appearance that a potential employer will remember.

Save your work, and keep the RESUME.WPD worksheet open to use in the next lesson.

The Underline icon works the same as the Bold and Italics icons, so you can underline text using the same steps that you used for bold and italics. You might be interested to know the keyboard shortcuts for the Bold and Italics features. The keyboard shortcuts are Ctrl+B for Bold, Ctrl+I for Italics, and Ctrl+U for Underline. To use the shortcuts, select the text first; then press the shortcut keys.

Lesson 3: Moving and Copying Text

After enhancing text, the most important skill you can learn is how to move and copy text. How many times have you written a paragraph and then decided you need to reorder the sentences? What about putting a phrase at the bottom of the page, only to wish you could move it to the top?

Now that you have improved the appearance of the resume by adding bold and italics to the text, take a look at the content and organization of the text to see if you can make any improvements. In this lesson, you move the Education section above the Work Experience because this order more accurately reflects the most recent accomplishment.

To Move and Copy Text

1 In the file RESUME.WPD, select the EDUCATION heading and the three lines underneath it, including one blank line (see figure 3.7).

You use the Select feature to tell WordPerfect what you want to move or copy. In this case, you want to move the EDUCATION section.

Figure 3.7
The resume with the EDUCATION section selected.

Click here to cut the section

Select the EDUCATION section

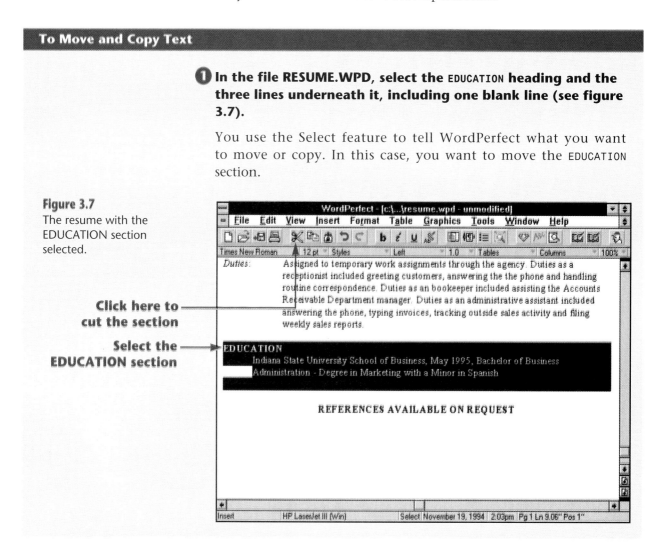

② Click the Cut icon.

The EDUCATION section has been moved to the Clipboard, which stores the text temporarily so you can paste it.

③ Position the insertion point at the beginning of the WORK EXPERIENCE line.

You need to position the insertion point right where you want the new section to appear—in this case, before the WORK EXPERIENCE section.

④ Click the Paste icon.

When you paste the EDUCATION section, the WORK EXPERIENCE section moves down to accommodate the change (see Figure 3.8).

Figure 3.8
The EDUCATION section now precedes the WORK EXPERIENCE section.

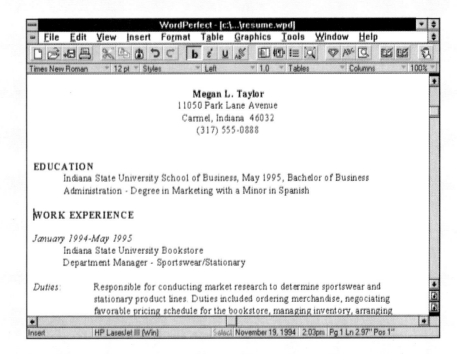

⑤ Select the last sentence in the Duties description for the temporary agency.

The sentence describing the experience as an administrative assistant needs to be placed before the sentence describing the experience as a bookkeeper.

⑥ Click the Cut icon.

⑦ Position the insertion point at the beginning of the third sentence in the description.

Again, because you want to position the sentence about the administrative assistant experience (presently the last sentence) *in front of*

continues

To Move and Copy Text (continued)

the sentence about the experience as a bookkeeper (presently the third sentence), you need to position the insertion point *at the beginning* of the third sentence.

❽ **Click the Paste icon.**

The third and last sentences of the description have been reordered. The new order matches the order of the assignments accepted through the temporary agency.

The sample resume should now look similar to Figure 3.9. Save your work and keep the RESUME.WPD file open to use in the next lesson, where you learn how to undo changes you have made.

Figure 3.9
The sample resume with the revised description for temporary office work.

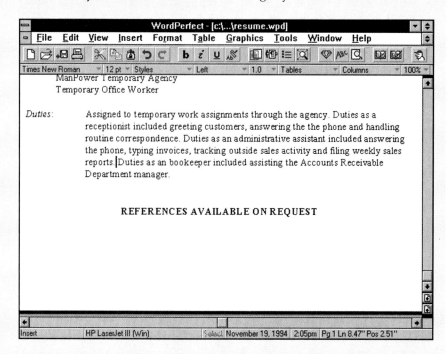

Jargon Watch

WordPerfect uses the terms **cut**, **copy**, and **paste** to describe moving and copying text. (You find each of these commands on the **E**dit menu). When you cut text, you take the text out of its present location. When you copy text, you leave the text alone—you just make a copy so that you can put that copy somewhere else. When you paste, you insert the cut or copied text to a new location.

The Windows **Clipboard** is an area in memory reserved for text that you cut and copy. Because it's a Windows feature, the Clipboard is available to all Windows applications. When you cut or copy a section of text, the text stays in the Clipboard so that you can paste it into a new location. Because the text remains in the Clipboard until you copy or cut a new item, you can paste it repeatedly to different locations.

When you copy text, you use the same steps as you use to cut text. The only difference is that you click the Copy icon instead of the Cut icon.

Word also offers several text editing shortcuts. First, you can click and drag selected text to a new location. If you click and drag, you move the selected text. If you hold down Ctrl while dragging, you copy the selected text. Of course, you can also use several keyboard shortcut keys. Table 3.1 lists the shortcuts you can use to select, cut, copy, and paste text.

Table 3.1 Keyboard Shortcuts to Cut, Copy and Paste Text	
Shortcut	Function
⇧Shift+Arrow Key	Selects text
⇧Shift+ Del or Ctrl+ X	Cuts text
Ctrl+ Ins or Ctrl+ C	Copies text
⇧Shift+ Ins or Ctrl+ V	Pastes text

Lesson 4: Using the Undo Feature

The Undo feature reverses the actions that you take on a document. For example, if you accidentally rearrange the wrong paragraph, or assign the wrong formatting command, the Undo feature lets you correct your mistake. Undo works for virtually every action you can take on a document—formatting, deleting, sorting, placing graphics, and so forth.

For this lesson, you *accidentally* paste text into the middle of a description; then you use the Undo feature to correct the error.

To Use the Undo Feature

❶ In the file RESUME.WPD, select the section for The Indiana State University Record—from the dates down to the last line of the description.

You copy this section, and then paste it into the wrong location.

❷ Click the Copy icon.

The selected text doesn't change because this time you have copied text, not moved it. WordPerfect has made a copy of the text and saved it to the Clipboard so that you can paste it somewhere else.

❸ Position the insertion point between the words the and bookstore in the Duties section of the University Bookstore section (see Figure 3.10).

continues

To Spell Check a Document (continued)

❸ Choose Replace.

Spell Check stops on the next word (ManPower) because of the irregular capitalization. The Suggestions list box contains the word in all lowercase, all uppercase, and initial caps. This company name, however, uses the irregular capitalization of the word, so you don't want to choose a replacement. Choose to ignore this word for the rest of the Spell Check session.

❹ Choose Skip Always.

Spell Check then stops on the next error, a duplicate word (the the). A single occurrence of the word automatically appears in the Replace **W**ith text box. Read the phrase carefully before you choose to remove the duplicate word—in some cases, it is grammatically correct to have duplicate words. In this case, you want to delete the second occurrence of the word.

❺ Choose Replace.

The next mistake is another misspelled word (bookeeper). Spell Check suggests two replacement words (bookkeeper and beekeeper). To select a replacement word, click the word, or use the arrow keys to move the selection bar to another word. This action moves the replacement word to the Replace **W**ith text box. In this case, the correct spelling (bookkeeper) already appears in the Replace **W**ith text box.

❻ Choose Replace.

Choosing Replace corrects the misspelling in the word bookeeper. When Spell Check finishes, a message dialog box appears stating that the Spell Check has been completed and asking if you want to close Spell Checker.

❼ Choose Yes.

Save your work and keep the RESUME.WPD file open to use in the next lesson, where you learn to use the Thesaurus.

When you start Spell Check, the program checks the whole document by default; however, you can change these settings. For example, if you have to edit a long document and you only want to spell check the area you have made changes to, select the text first; then start Spell Check. On the second pass through a document, Spell Check only checks the areas of the document that have changed since the first pass. You can also spell check a word, which lets you verify the accuracy of the word without having to run Spell Check on the whole document.

Lesson 6: Using the Thesaurus

For those times when you need just the right word to describe something, WordPerfect has a Thesaurus program. This program also comes in handy if you discover that you have used the same word repeatedly in your document and you want to find a substitute. The Thesaurus program lists synonyms (words with similar meanings) and antonyms (words with opposite meanings) for a selected word. Try using the Thesaurus now.

To Use the Thesaurus

1 In the file RESUME.WPD, position the insertion point on the word ordering **in the second line of the first description.**

This action identifies the word you want to look up. You can also start Thesaurus from a blank screen.

2 From the Tools menu, choose Thesaurus.

The Thesaurus dialog box opens with a list of synonyms and antonyms for the word ordering, as shown in Figure 3.12. The Thesaurus organizes the suggestions by category: verbs, nouns, adjectives, and antonyms.

Figure 3.12
The Thesaurus dialog box with a list of synonyms and antonyms.

(n) stands for nouns

Words with dots next to them are headwords

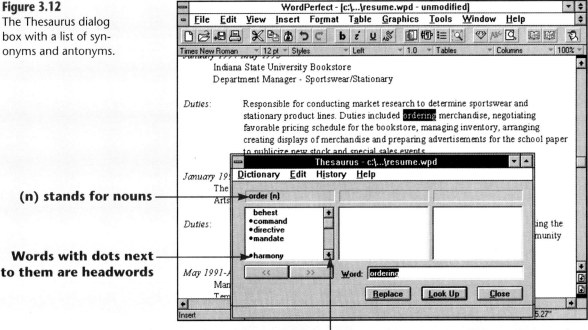

Scroll through the list of words

Headwords have a small dot next to the words—these words have their own list of synonyms and antonyms that you can open up and look through.

continues

To Use the Grammar Checker   (continued)

Grammatik detects the first problem in the description for the University Bookstore. The error relates to the word schedule. Note that this word is spelled correctly, so Spell Check did not see the error. A grammar check, however, checks for more than just spelling, detecting errors in sentence structure.

By coincidence, the dialog box is hiding the sentence with the problem. As with most dialog boxes in Windows applications, you can click and drag the title bar to move the dialog box out of the way.

2 Click and drag the title bar of the Grammatik dialog box.

Moving the dialog box out of the way lets you see the highlighted word schedule. After reviewing the sentence and the suggestions made by Grammatik, you should replace the word schedule with schedules. Because the word appears at the top of the list of replacements, this word is already selected for you.

3 Choose Replace.

The next problem Grammatik identifies is in the date format used for the resume. Grammatical rules state that a date should be written out in a month, day, year format. In a resume, however, the days don't matter—only the month and year. Choose to skip the date format rule for the rest of the document.

4 Choose Skip Always.

The next problem Grammatik identifies was also found by the Spell Check—the irregular capitalization in the company name ManPower. The company name is accurate as written, so you can skip this problem and move to the next one.

5 Choose Skip Always.

Grammatik has located a problem with an article (an) in the last description. The Grammatik program suggests that you replace an with a. Because the a is the only replacement in the list, it already appears selected for you.

6 Choose Replace.

When Grammatik finishes checking the document, a message dialog box appears asking if you want to close Grammatik.

7 Choose Yes to close Grammatik.

The changes you have made to your sample resume in this project have improved the quality of this important document. Save your work, and print two copies of RESUME.WPD, one to keep and one to turn in. Close RESUME.WPD after printing. If you have completed your session on the computer, exit WordPerfect for Windows and the Windows Program Manager before turning off the computer. Otherwise, continue with the "Applying Your Skills" case studies at the end of this project.

Checking Your Skills

True/False

For each of the following statements, check *T* or *F* to indicate whether the statement is true or false.

__T __F **1.** The Spell Check program proofs your document for errors in word usage.

__T __F **2.** Moving a section of text is a two-step process: cut and paste.

__T __F **3.** A single mouse click on a word selects the word.

__T __F **4.** The Grammatik program stops on misspelled words.

__T __F **5.** The Undo feature reverses the last action taken on a document.

Multiple Choice

Circle the letter of the correct answer for each of the following.

1. The Spell Check program looks for _____.

    a. misspelled words

    b. duplicate words

    c. irregular capitalization

    d. all the above

2. _____ selects a sentence.

    a. Triple-clicking a paragraph

    b. Clicking the left margin area

    c. Double-clicking a sentence

    d. Holding down Ctrl, then clicking the sentence

3. Which menu contains the Thesaurus option?

    a. Tools

    b. Edit

    c. Format

    d. File

4. In the Thesaurus, headwords are indicated by a(n) _____.

    a. asterisk

    b. small dot

    c. check mark

    d. small box

5. C̲trl̲+ B̲J̲ is the shortcut key for which feature?

   a. Italics

   b. Spell Check

   c. Boldface

   d. Undo

Completion

In the blank provided, write the correct answer for each of the following statements.

1. To move a section of text, you must _____ the text first.

2. If you accidentally assign the wrong formatting to your document, use the _____ feature to put things back the way they were.

3. The Thesaurus displays lists of _____ and _____ for a word.

4. The **P**aste command _____ text at the insertion point.

5. Both the _____ program and the _____ program have dictionaries.

Applying Your Skills

Take a few minutes to practice the skills you have learned in this project by completing the "On Your Own" and "Brief Cases" case studies.

On Your Own

Preparing Your Resume

Now that you have some experience working with the editing tools in WordPerfect, you can create your own resume. You can use the sample resume as a guide, but feel free to be creative with the arrangement of the elements in your resume. Use the Bold, Italics, and Underline features to enhance the appearance and make your headings stand out. The Indent key (F7̲J̲) is used after the Duties headings (in the sample resume) to indent the description, and T̲ab̲:̲ is used to indent the company names and job titles under the dates.

To Create Your Resume

1. Start Windows; then start WordPerfect for Windows.

2. In the new document WordPerfect has ready for you when you start the program, type a draft copy of your resume.

3. Go back and enhance sections of the text with boldface, italics, and underline.

4. If necessary, rearrange the elements to best communicate your experience and unique qualities.

5. Use the Spell Check program to check your document for spelling errors.

6. Use the Thesaurus program to help suggest words that clearly convey your meaning.

7. Use the Grammatik program to proof your document for grammatical mistakes.

8. Save the resume as **MYRESUME.WPD,** and print a copy.

Brief Cases

Editing and Proofing Ad Copy

In Project 3, you learned how to select and enhance text, and how to use the WordPerfect writing tools to proofread your documents. Use the skills you have learned to edit the ad copy you created in Project 2.

To Edit and Proof The Ad Copy

1. Open the ADCOPY.WPD file, and save it as **ADFINAL.WPD**.

2. Consider changing the order of sentences in the description of the store to place more emphasis on the location than on the wide selection.

3. Run Spell Check to proof the document for spelling errors, duplicate words or irregular capitalization.

4. Use the Thesaurus to help find just the right words for your description.

5. Run the Grammatik program to make sure the ad copy is grammatically correct.

Project

4

Formatting Documents

Formatting a Research Paper

In this project, you learn how to

> Change Margins

> Change Line Spacing

> Change Justification

> Indent Text

> Insert Page Numbers

> Insert Page Breaks

> Change the Font and Font Size

> Insert a Header

Why Would I Do This?

Now that you have some experience creating and editing documents, you can learn how to format documents. WordPerfect has a set of standard format settings already in place, which allow you to create many basic documents without changing any settings. To create a more professional-looking document, however, you can change the standard settings.

Simple changes like different margins and line spacing can make a document easier to read. Page numbers and headers provide important information for the reader. One of the most popular enhancements, changing the font and font size, can improve the appearance of any document.

Lesson 1: Changing Margins

Document margins determine how much white space a document has around the text. When necessary, you can specify left, right, top, and bottom margins. WordPerfect has preset margins of one inch (the standard for most business documents) on all sides so that you can create many documents without changing the margins.

A section of a research paper has been provided for your use in this project, so open the file to begin editing.

To Change Margins

❶ **Open the PROJ0401.WPD file; then save it as REPORT.WPD.**

WordPerfect opens the report in a new document window. You can now begin formatting the sample report (see Figure 4.1).

Figure 4.1
The sample report open in a document window.

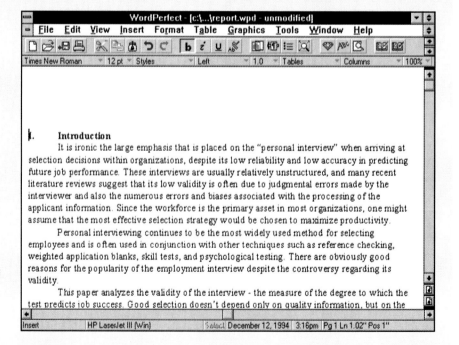

Before you open the Format menu, make sure the insertion point appears where you want the formatting change to begin. Because you want to change the top and bottom margins for the entire document, the insertion point should be placed at the top of the document. When you open a document, however, WordPerfect places the insertion point at the top of the document, so you don't need to move it now.

② Choose Format from the menu bar; then choose Margins.

The Margins dialog box opens (see Figure 4.2). A sample page appears so that you can preview your margin changes before you apply them to the document.

Figure 4.2
The Margins dialog box.

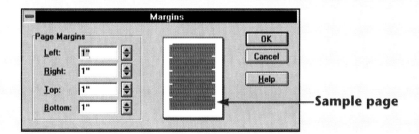

—**Sample page**

❸ Double-click the Top text box.

When you double-click the **T**op text box, the current setting of 1" appears highlighted. When a setting appears highlighted, you can enter the new setting, and that text automatically replaces the selected setting. Click the up and down arrows to increase or decrease the setting if you prefer.

❹ Type 1.25.

This action sets the top margin to an inch and a quarter. Notice how the sample page changes to show you how the margin you selected will look. Now, change the bottom margin to an inch and a quarter.

❺ Double-click the Bottom text box, and type 1.25.

The sample page now shows you how the new top and bottom margins will look when you apply them to the text.

❻ Choose OK.

The new margins have been applied to the document text, and WordPerfect has automatically repaginated the text accordingly.

Save your work and keep the REPORT.WPD file open to use in the next lesson, where you learn to change the line spacing.

Lesson 2: Changing Line Spacing

As you may have noticed when you created your cover letter in Project 2, WordPerfect uses single spacing on all new documents. You can change the amount of spacing between lines with the Line Spacing feature. Try changing the line spacing for the research paper to double-spacing now.

To Change Line Spacing

① In the REPORT.WPD file, position your insertion point at the top of the document.

The insertion point should appear at the beginning of the title line—I. Introduction. The simplest way to change the line spacing is with the Line Spacing button on the Power Bar.

② Click the Line Spacing button.

The Line Spacing drop-down list, shown in Figure 4.3, has the three most frequently used line spacing settings (1.0, 1.5, 2.0) and an Other option, which opens the Line Spacing dialog box. You can specify another value in this dialog box.

Figure 4.3
The Line Spacing
drop-down list.

Line Spacing
drop-down list

Line Spacing button

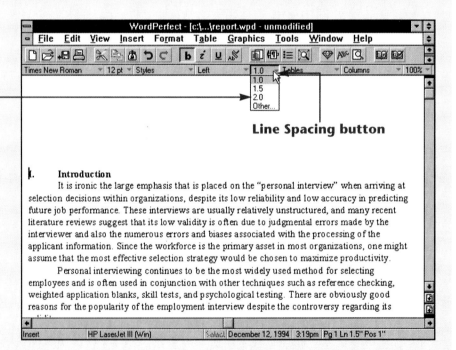

③ Choose 2.0.

Choosing the 2.0 setting is the equivalent of choosing double-spacing for the document. Use the arrow keys or the scroll bar to scroll through the document so that you can see the results of the change.

Save your work and keep the REPORT.WPD file open to use in the next lesson, where you learn to change the justification.

Lesson 3: Changing Justification

Justification

The alignment of multiple lines of text along the left margin, right margin, or between both margins.

Justification describes how text aligns between the left and right margins. Left justification is the most commonly used setting, so WordPerfect uses left justification as the default setting. Table 4.1 (page 74) provides a description of the five types of justification.

Now try changing the justification for the research paper.

To Change Justification

❶ In the REPORT.WPD file, position the insertion point at the top of the document.

Because you want to change the justification for the whole document, you need to position the insertion point at the top of the document. Now, change the justification to Full using the Justification button on the Power Bar.

❷ Click the Justification button.

The drop-down list for the Justification button appears (see Figure 4.4).

Figure 4.4

The Justification button drop-down list.

Justification drop-down list

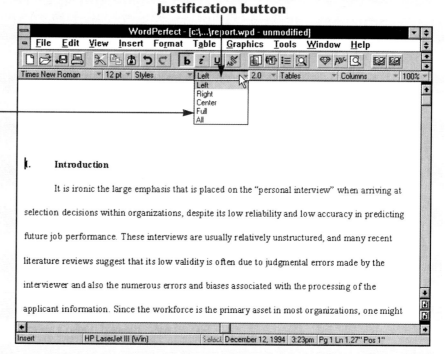

❸ Choose Full from the drop-down list.

When you choose full justification, WordPerfect inserts a small amount of space between each character to create a smooth right margin. The report text should now be fully justified with smooth left and right margins (see Figure 4.5).

continues

To Create the Proposal

1. Open the file PROJ0402.WPD, and save it as **LOANPRP.WPD**.

2. Choose an interesting font face from your list and change the font face for the text of the proposal.

3. Insert page numbers at the bottom right corner of every page.

4. Insert a header with the name of your proposal and the date you will be making your presentation. Use a smaller font size for the text of the header.

5. Change the top and bottom margins to **1.25"**.

6. Change the justification to Full for the body text.

7. Set the line spacing for the proposal to **1.5**.

8. Save your work, and print two copies of the file.

Brief Cases

Create an Annual Report

Use the skills you have learned in this project to create an annual report for the investors of Sound Byte Music. The report should include sales figures from fiscal year 1995 and projections for fiscal year 1996. The report should also include future expansion plans, proposed budget figures, and a new advertising schedule. Present this information in an easy-to-read format.

To Create the Annual Report

1. Open the file PROJ0403.WPD, and save it as **ANUALRPT.WPD**.

2. Create a striking title page by using an attractive font and larger font sizes.

3. Create the header with the name of the report and the date it was prepared. Use a smaller font size for the text of the header.

4. Insert page numbers at the bottom center of the page.

5. Change the justification to Full and set up the report to be double-spaced.

6. Create headings for the pages that will contain the financial information and advertising schedules.

7. Save your work, and then print two copies of the document.

Project

5

Preparing Long Documents

Enhancing a Research Paper

In this project, you learn how to

- Search for Text
- Replace Text
- Create and Edit Footnotes
- Create a Cross-Reference
- Select Text for a Table of Contents
- Create and Generate a Table of Contents Page

Why Would I Do This?

Long documents such as research papers include special features to make locating information within documents easier for the reader. A table of contents gives readers an idea of the topics you cover in the document. Footnotes provide documentation of the sources you used. Cross-references direct the reader to a related item within the document.

You may not have to create long documents very often, but when you do have to write a term paper or business report, the long document features of WordPerfect provide an easy way to enhance your work.

Lesson 1: Searching for Text

The Find feature helps you locate specific words or phrases quickly and easily. Searching for a word by reading the entire document is often time-consuming and error-prone, especially in long, complex documents. WordPerfect's Find feature searches the entire document and highlights every instance of the word you seek.

To Search for Text

1 Open the PROJ0501.WPD file, and save it as INTRVIEW.WPD.

2 Choose Edit; then choose Find and Replace.

The Find and Replace Text dialog box appears (see Figure 5.1).

Figure 5.1
The Find and Replace Text dialog box.

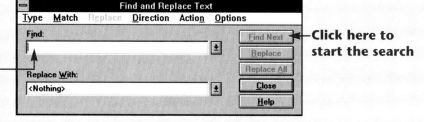

Type the text you want to find here

Click here to start the search

3 Type Diboye in the Find text box.

In the text, the correct spelling should be Dipboye. You suspect that this name has been misspelled throughout the report.

4 Click Find Next.

This action starts the search. WordPerfect begins comparing every word in the document (including the footnote text) with the text that you typed in the Find text box. When the program finds a match, it stops, and then highlights the word (see Figure 5.2).

Figure 5.2
WordPerfect has located a match for the text you typed in the Find text box.

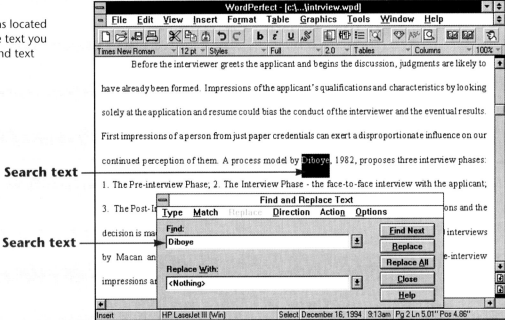

Search text

Search text

⑤ Choose Find Next.

Choosing **F**ind Next continues the search through the document for Diboye. As suspected, the name has been incorrectly spelled throughout the document. Notice that the next occurrence of Diboye is in a footnote. Because the insertion point now appears in the footnote area of the document, you need to move out of that area before you can move to the top of the document and start the next lesson.

⑥ Scroll upwards until you can see the text of the report; then click inside the text.

Now that the insertion point is out of the footnote area, you can move to the top of the document.

⑦ Press Ctrl+Home.

Notice that you don't have to close the Find and Replace dialog box to reposition the insertion point. In case you want to make a manual correction, you can click inside the document, make the correction, and then continue the **F**ind operation.

⑧ Choose Close.

Choosing **C**lose closes the dialog box. In the next lesson, you use the Replace feature to perform a search and replace so that you can correct every occurrence of the incorrect spelling.

Because you haven't made any changes to the INTRVIEW.WPD file during this lesson, you don't need to save the file now. Leave the document open so that you can use it in the next lesson.

Lesson 5: Selecting Text for a Table of Contents

A table of contents provides readers with a guide to the topics covered in a long document. WordPerfect makes creating a table of contents easy—all you have to do is select the text that you want to appear in the table, tell WordPerfect where it should appear in the table, and then generate the table. WordPerfect locates the text you have marked, identifies the page numbers for the marked text, and then builds the table of contents for you. As with cross-references, you need to remember to regenerate the table of contents after you make editing changes to the document so that WordPerfect can update the page numbers.

In this lesson, try creating a table of contents that lists all of the headings and subheadings in the research paper. The first step in creating a table of contents is selecting and marking the text that you want to appear in the table. Follow these steps to select text for a table of contents now.

To Select Text for a Table of Contents

❶ In the INTRVIEW.WPD file, press Ctrl + Home .

This action moves the insertion point to the top of the document where you can begin selecting text for the table.

❷ Choose Tools; then Table of Contents.

When you choose Table of **C**ontents, the Table of Contents feature bar appears below the Power Bar. This feature bar makes it easier for you to mark text for the different levels of the table. Now, you need to select the headings and mark them for the table.

❸ Select the first heading in the report—Introduction.

Make sure you only select the heading text and not the Roman numeral or the blank line underneath that text (see Figure 5.11). If you include the Roman numeral or the blank line, these items will appear in the Table of Contents. The Table of Contents feature automatically includes a blank line between entries.

If you have problems...

If you double-click the selection area or triple-click the heading, WordPerfect includes the blank line after the heading in the selection. You may find that the easiest method for selecting only the heading text is to start at the end of the heading; then click and drag to the left until you select the heading.

---

❹ Click the Mark 1 button on the Table of Contents feature bar.

Clicking the Mark **1** button marks this text for Level 1 in the table. Level 1 entries appear at the left margin when the Table of Contents is generated.

Figure 5.11
The Table of Contents feature bar makes it easy to mark text for the table.

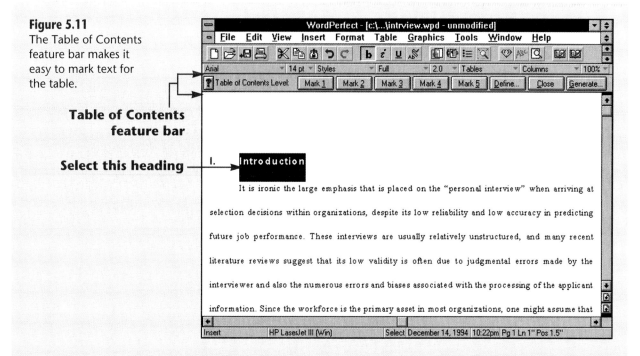

Table of Contents feature bar

Select this heading

❺ Select the next major heading—Pre-interview Impression Effects.

Because this heading is a major heading, it should have a Level 1 heading as well. All major headings receive the Level 1 heading.

❻ Click the Mark 1 button.

Clicking the Mark **1** button marks this heading for Level 1 in the table.

❼ Select the subheading Pre-interview Impressions.

Don't include the colon at the end of the heading when you select the text because if you do, the colon ends up in the Table of Contents. Here again, make sure you only select the text of the heading, not the blank line underneath. Click the end of the heading; then drag to the left until you have selected the heading (but not the Roman numeral).

❽ Click the Mark 2 button.

Clicking the Mark 2 button marks this text for Level 2 in the table. Level 2 entries appear indented half an inch from the left margin.

❾ Continue selecting the rest of the headings, marking the major headings (with Roman numerals) as Level 1 and the subheadings (with letters) as Level 2.

Marking the rest of the entries completes the preparation for creating the table of contents.

Save your work and keep the INTRVIEW.WPD file open to use in the next lesson. Also, leave the Table of Contents feature bar on the screen for the next lesson, where you create a page for the table of contents and then generate the table itself.

Lesson 6: Creating and Generating a Table of Contents Page

After you have selected the topics you want for the table of contents, you need to create a separate page for the table. Typically, a table of contents appears by itself on a page preceding the body of the research paper.

In this lesson, you create a new page for the table of contents and then add a heading for the table of contents page. After you choose the format for the different levels in the table, WordPerfect compiles the table of contents.

To Create and Generate a Table of Contents Page

① **In the INTRVIEW.WPD file, press** Ctrl+Home **twice.**

This action positions the insertion point at the very top of the document, right before any of the formatting codes for the first page.

② **Press** Ctrl+End**; then press** ↑**.**

Pressing Ctrl+End inserts a page break. Pressing ↑ moves the insertion point into the new page you just created. Now center a title for the table.

③ **Press** ⇧Shift+F7**.**

You could also choose Fo**r**mat, **L**ine, **C**enter from the menu. Although you can select text you have already typed and center it, it's easier to use this method to center a single line before typing it.

④ **Type Table of Contents, and press** ↵Enter **twice.**

You want to insert a blank line between the title and the page number heading.

⑤ **Press** Alt+F7**.**

You could also choose Fo**r**mat, **L**ine, **F**lush Right from the menu. Although you can select text you have already typed and align it against the right margin, it's easier to use this method to flush-right a single line before typing it.

⑥ **Type Page; then press** ↵Enter **twice.**

This heading should appear flush against the right margin, where the page numbers will appear when the table is complete.

The table of contents page should now look like Figure 5.12.

With the insertion point positioned where you want the table to start, you need to tell WordPerfect to build the table of contents.

⑦ **Click the Define button.**

The Define Table of Contents dialog box appears (see Figure 5.13).

Figure 5.12
The Table of Contents page.

Click here to define the table

Click here to generate the table

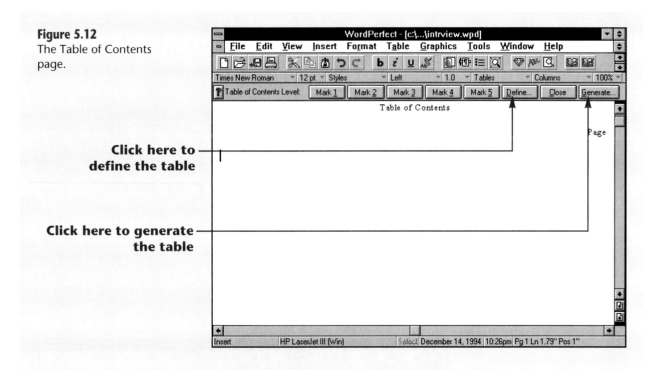

Figure 5.13
The Define Table of Contents dialog box.

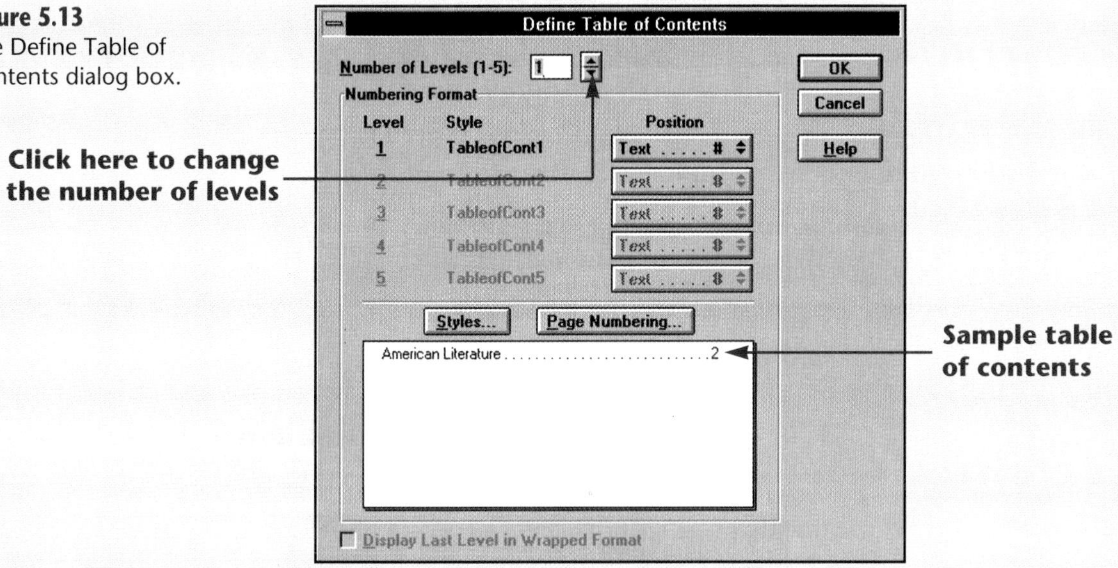

Click here to change the number of levels

Sample table of contents

❽ Click the up arrow next to Number of Levels.

Clicking the up arrow changes the number of levels to 2. Notice how the sample page at the bottom of the dialog box changes to show you what a two-level table looks like.

❾ Choose OK.

WordPerfect inserts a marker — << Table of Contents will generate here >> — to indicate where the table should appear.

The last step to creating a table of contents is generating the table. You used the Generate feature earlier when you created the

continues

Include a footnote that identifies the financial statements accompanying the report. Use a cross-reference to refer readers to 1995 figures when 1996 figures are presented with expansion plans and advertising budget. A table of contents should include all headings in the report.

To Add Items to the Annual Report

1. Open the file PROJO503.WPD, and save it as **ANULRPT2.WPD**.

2. Add a footnote to the 1995 figures referring back to the 1995 financial statements.

3. Add a footnote that identifies the financial statement as a source document for the report.

4. Add a cross-reference to the 1995 figures in the discussion about 1996 expansion plans and the proposed advertising campaign.

5. Select the headings and mark them for entry in the Table of Contents.

6. Create a Table of Contents page with a title and a page number heading.

7. Define the table of contents on the page you created.

8. Generate the table of contents and the cross-references.

9. Save your work, and print two copies of the file.

Project 6

Using Tables and Graphics

Completing a Newsletter

In this project, you learn how to

- Create a Table
- Enter Text into a Table
- Format a Table
- Calculate Values in a Table
- Insert a Graphic Line
- Insert a Graphic Image
- Move and Resize a Graphic Image

Why Would I Do This?

The Tables feature is one of the most versatile and easy-to-use features in the program. Although you use the Tables feature in many ways, people most often use this feature for information that needs to be formatted into columns. You could use the Columns feature to accomplish this task, but the Tables feature is easier to use and has more options for formatting the information and the table itself. In fact, a Tables Expert tool lets you assign complex formatting with just a few mouse clicks. The Tables feature also has over 90 built-in spreadsheet functions, which allow you to perform most of the tasks that a spreadsheet program does—using WordPerfect.

Graphics can also be added to your documents to illustrate a point, to add excitement, or to add creative flair. In WordPerfect, you can add graphic lines and images to your documents. Horizontal graphic lines can separate letterheads, mastheads, headers, or footers from the rest of the text. Vertical lines often divide and delineate columns of text. Thousands of images, called clip art, are available through software stores, mail order catalogs, and on-line services. In fact, WordPerfect includes a wide variety of clip art that you can use in formal and informal documents.

You use tables and graphics in this project to put the finishing touches on a newsletter for the members of the Rollerblading Club.

Lesson 1: Creating a Table

The WordPerfect Tables feature is very similar to spreadsheet software, such as Excel, both in the structure and in the terminology. Both spreadsheets and WordPerfect Tables are comprised of a grid of columns and rows. You can leave the lines in and format them to suit your needs, or you can take them out so they won't print. When you create a table, you need to estimate how many columns and how many rows (or lines) you will need. Try creating a table in WordPerfect now.

To Create a Table

❶ Open the PROJ0601.WPD file, and save it as NEWSLTR.WPD.

WordPerfect opens the partially completed newsletter into a new document window (see Figure 6.1).

Figure 6.1
The sample newsletter.

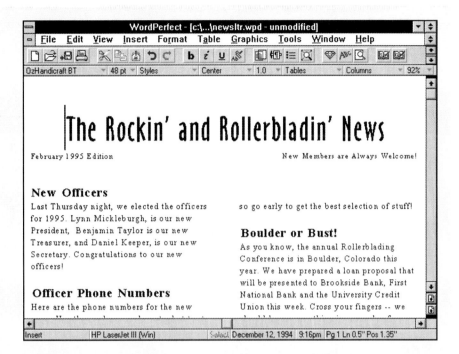

2 **Position the insertion point on the blank line above the heading** Weekend Roll.

You want to create the table for the officer phone numbers in this spot.

3 **Click the Tables button on the Power Bar.**

As you click, you need to hold down the mouse button. When you do this, WordPerfect displays an empty grid. You have to click and drag the mouse to highlight the number of rows and columns you need. Drag the mouse slowly until you get the hang of it.

4 **Click and drag the mouse over and down until the top of the grid reads** 2 x 3; **then release the mouse button.**

The 2 represents the number of columns; the 3 represents the number of rows. Make sure you have 2 columns and 3 rows selected.

If you have problems...

If you have problems clicking and dragging across the grid, click the Undo icon on the Toolbar, and try again. The Undo feature reverses the last action you take on a document—in this case, creating a table.

You can also use the **T**able menu to create a table. Choose **T**able; then choose **C**reate. The Create Table dialog box appears. Select the **C**olumns and **R**ows options under the Table Size section to specify 2 columns and 3 rows. Choose OK to create the table.

continues

WordPerfect creates the table at the insertion point. Notice how the table is created within the margins of the newsletter column and that both columns of the table have the same width. By default, WordPerfect creates evenly spaced columns between the available margin space. You can easily change the column widths, if necessary. Your newsletter should now look like Figure 6.2.

Figure 6.2
The sample newsletter with the table.

Click here to create a table

Table

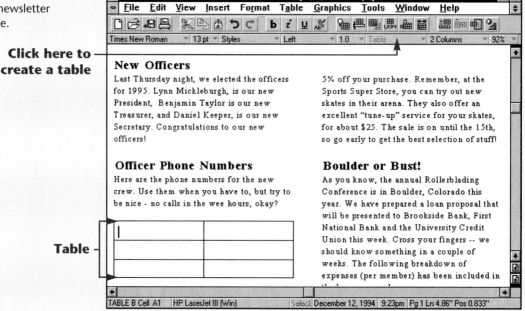

❺ **Scroll down until you can see the whole table on-screen.**

The default table has a single line between the columns and rows and around the outside border. You will change the table lines with the Table Expert later in the project.

Save your work and keep the NEWSLTR.WPD file open to use in the next lesson, where you learn to enter text into a table.

Jargon Watch

Tables are composed of rows and columns. The intersection of a row and a column is called a **cell**. In spreadsheets, **rows** are numbered from top to bottom and **columns** are labeled with letters from left to right. In addition, each cell has a unique address, called a **cell address**. A cell address is composed of the column letter, followed by the row number. For example, the top left cell is A1.

Lesson 2: Enter Text into a Table

Typing text into a table works the same as typing text into the document window, with only a few differences. One difference is that you use [Tab↹] and [⇧Shift]+[Tab↹] to move between the cells of a table. [Tab↹] moves you one cell to the right; [⇧Shift]+[Tab↹] moves you one cell to the left. When you type information into a cell, the text wraps within the margins of the cell so that you don't have to worry about the cell size. Each cell expands to accommodate the text that you enter. You can't, however, make one cell larger than one page.

In the newsletter document, you need to type each officer's name in the first column and the officer's phone number in the second column. Try entering text in the table now.

The insertion point already appears in the first cell (WordPerfect puts it there when you create the table), so you can start typing the first entry.

To Enter Text into a Table

❶ In the NEWSLTR.WPD file, type Rebecca Smith-Bailey.

You enter the new president's name first, followed by her phone number.

❷ Press [Tab↹].

Pressing [Tab↹] moves you one cell to the right. You type Rebecca's phone number here.

❸ Type 581-3731.

Unless you change the alignment, WordPerfect aligns the text against the left side of the cell. As you will see later, you can align text in the center, on the right, or by decimal points.

❹ Press [Tab↹].

When you press [Tab↹] in the last cell of a row, your insertion point moves down to the first cell in the next row.

❺ Type Benjamin Taylor; then press [Tab↹].

The new treasurer's name appears in the second row.

❻ Type 581-4415; then press [Tab↹].

Your insertion point should now be positioned in the first cell of the last row.

❼ Type Daniel Keeper; then press [Tab↹].

The new secretary's name appears in the last row.

continues

To Enter Text into a Table (continued)

❽ Type 581-1150.

Don't press [Tab⤒] again—if you do, WordPerfect automatically creates a new row, which you don't need. Your table should now look like Figure 6.3.

Figure 6.3
The completed table with names and phone numbers.

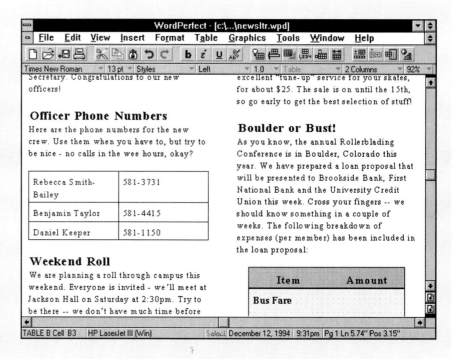

Save your work and keep the NEWSLTR.WPD file open to use in the next lesson, where you learn to format a table.

You can also use the mouse to position the insertion point inside a table. To move the insertion point to a specific cell, position the mouse pointer on the cell, and click the left mouse button.

Lesson 3: Formatting a Table

When you create a new table, WordPerfect uses a number of default format settings. As mentioned, single lines appear inside the table and form the outside border; the text is justified against the left side of the cell, and the columns have equal widths. At times, you may need to adjust the width of the columns to accommodate the cell contents. In this case, you increase the size of the left column so the full name of the president fits on one line. The Table Expert feature enables you to adjust the format of your table using preset templates.

Now try using the Table Expert to change the outside table border to a double line and to adjust the column widths.

❶ In the NEWSLTR.WPD file, position the mouse pointer on the vertical line between the first and second columns.

When you position the mouse pointer on this line, the mouse pointer changes to a double vertical line with arrows on either side (see Figure 6.4). You use this *sizing pointer* to adjust the width of the columns.

Figure 6.4
The mouse pointer adjusts the column widths in the table.

Sizing pointer ——

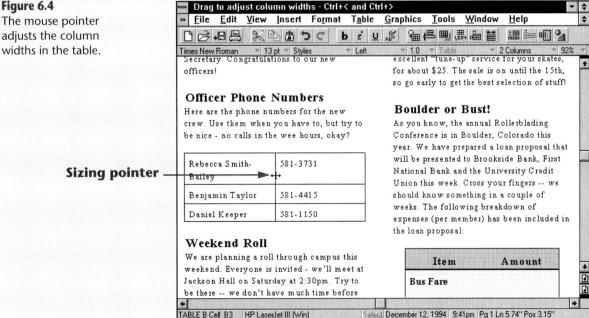

❷ Click and drag the sizing pointer to the right.

When you click and drag the sizing pointer, a dotted guideline, running from the ruler down to the status line, appears. As you drag the mouse, this line helps you see the new column width. You need to increase the size of the left column so that the officers' full names fit on one line (about a quarter of an inch).

❸ Release the mouse button.

Releasing the mouse button clears the guideline and adjusts the width of the columns. Your table should now look like Figure 6.5.

continues

To Format a Table   (continued)

Figure 6.5
Resizing the left column allows more room for the officer name.

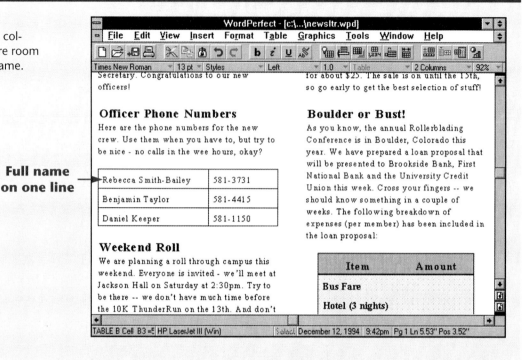

Full name on one line

If you have problems...

If the name (Rebecca Smith-Bailey) still won't fit on one line, click and drag the vertical line farther to the right. Make sure you wait until the sizing pointer appears before you click and drag the vertical line.

4 **Position the insertion point inside the first cell of the table.**

 5 **Click the Table Expert icon on the Toolbar.**

The Table Expert dialog box appears (see Figure 6.6). A list of available styles appears down the left side of the dialog box. When you choose a style, the sample table changes to reflect the formatting options for that style.

6 **Press ↓ several times.**

Take a minute and scroll through the list so you can see the variety of styles available.

7 **Select Single Double Border in the list of Available Styles.**

The sample table shows you what this style looks like when assigned.

Figure 6.6
The Table Expert dialog box.

Click here to select a different style ▶

Use this scroll bar ▶ to move through the list of styles

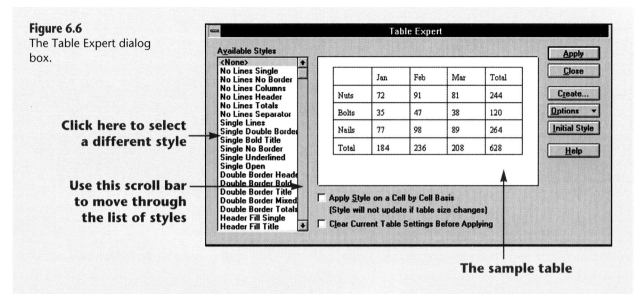

The sample table

❽ Choose Apply.

Choosing **A**pply assigns the selected style to the table. Your table should now look like Figure 6.7.

Figure 6.7
The table with the double-line border style.

Double-line ▶ border

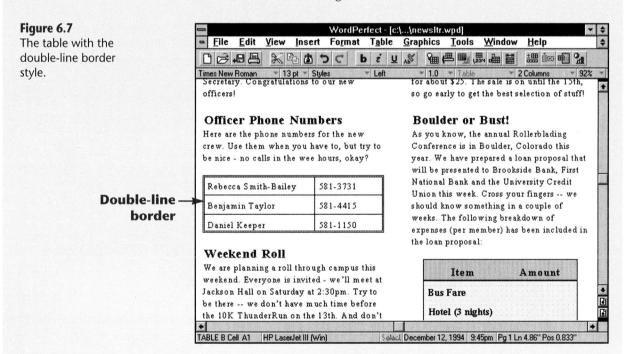

Save your work and keep the NEWSLTR.WPD file open to use in the next lesson, where you learn to calculate values in a table.

In this lesson, you used the mouse to resize the columns so that the president's full name would fit on one line. You can also use the Size Column to Fit on the QuickMenu to accomplish this task. Simply position the insertion point inside the column you want to resize, click the right mouse button, and choose Size Column to Fit.

In addition, the Toolbar has a Size Column to Fit icon that you can click after positioning the insertion point in the column you want to resize.

The Table Format icon on the Toolbar opens the Format dialog box, which enables you to choose formatting options for a cell (or selected cells), a row, a column, or the entire table. From this dialog box, you can choose a variety of formatting options for the table.

Lesson 4: Calculating Values in a Table

Value
A numeric cell entry.

The WordPerfect Tables feature includes an extensive list of built-in functions, similar to those found in a spreadsheet program. You can perform extremely complex calculations on figures using a table. The most common calculation, the Sum formula, adds *values* together to produce a total.

The table at the bottom of the newsletter shows expenses for the Rollerblading Club's trip to Colorado. The first column lists the expense items for the trip; the second column will hold the dollar amount for each item. Try entering values and calculating a total in the table now.

To Calculate Values in a Table

❶ In the NEWSLTR.WPD file, position the insertion point in the second row of the second column in the expense table.

The insertion point appears in cell B2. Notice the new indicator on the far left side of the status line shows the name of the table and the cell address of the cell that currently contains the insertion point.

❷ Type 125; then press ⬇.

This table already has the formatting for the number type set to Fixed (2 decimal places), so WordPerfect automatically inserts the decimal point and the decimal places each time you enter a whole number. Pressing ⬇ moves you down to the next row in the column.

❸ Type 75.5; then press ⬇.

In this figure, you have typed in the decimal point and one decimal place. WordPerfect fills in the second decimal place for you. If this figure had been a round number (like 75), you wouldn't have had to type either of the decimal places.

4 Type 100; then press ↓.

5 Type 35; then press ↓.

The table should now look like the one shown in Figure 6.8.

Figure 6.8
The table with the expense figures entered.

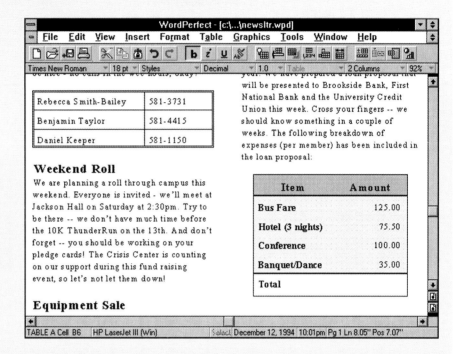

The insertion point should now appear in cell B6. You want the total amount to appear in this cell so you will insert the formula here. The fastest way to insert the Sum formula in a cell is to use the Table QuickMenu. You can access QuickMenus throughout the program by pressing the right mouse button.

6 Position the mouse pointer inside the table.

To access the Table QuickMenu, both the insertion point and mouse pointer have to be positioned inside a table.

7 Click and hold down the right mouse button.

The Table QuickMenu appears (see Figure 6.9). Make sure you hold down the mouse button, or the QuickMenu may disappear.

continues

To Calculate Values in a Table (continued)

Figure 6.9
The Table QuickMenu.

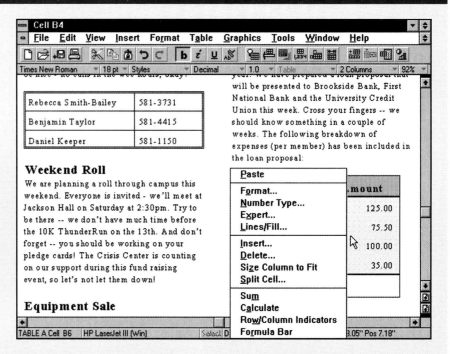

❽ Drag the mouse down until you select the Sum option; then release the mouse button.

The QuickMenu clears, and the Sum formula is inserted in the table cell. When you insert a new formula, WordPerfect automatically calculates the formula at that time, so the total amount of the expenses is calculated for you.

Notice that the total amount appears larger and has a dollar sign in front of it. This figure has been formatted with the Large font attribute and the Currency number type. Your table should now look like Figure 6.10.

Figure 6.10
The expense table with the total amount calculated.

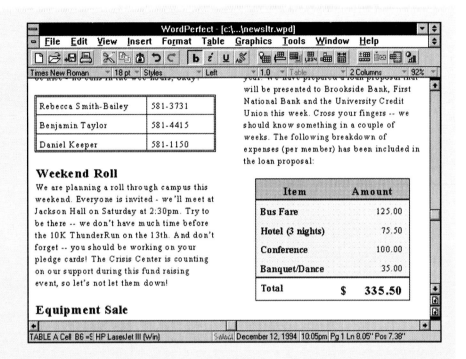

Save your work and keep the NEWSLTR.WPD file open to use in the next lesson, where you learn to insert a graphic line.

If you have problems...

If you have problems with the QuickMenu, you can insert the Sum formula using the Table menu by choosing Table, Sum. You can also press Ctrl+= if you prefer the keyboard shortcut.

Although the contents of cell B6 are a Sum formula, the results of the formula are shown in the cell. Spreadsheet programs work the same way. You can enter a calculation (2+2) in a cell, and the *results* of that calculation (4) appear in the cell, not the calculation itself.

If you change any of the figures involved in a formula or alter a formula, you need to recalculate the table. You can choose Calculate from the Table menu and the Table QuickMenu to accomplish this task.

Lesson 5: Inserting a Graphic Line

You can create horizontal (left to right) and vertical (top to bottom) graphic lines in WordPerfect. The **G**raphics menu (see Figure 6.11) has **H**orizontal and **V**ertical Line options that quickly create a basic thin line. WordPerfect also has a Custom **L**ine option that lets you create fancier lines with varying thickness and line combinations.

Masthead
The section of a newsletter that includes the title, date, and special messages.

In the sample newsletter, create a custom line below the heading (also called a *masthead*) now.

1 **In the NEWSLTR.WPD file, position the insertion point on the line below the heading lines (see Figure 6.11).**

You want to create the horizontal line here.

2 **Choose Graphics.**

The **G**raphics menu appears (see Figure 6.11).

Figure 6.11
The **G**raphics menu.

Position the insertion point here

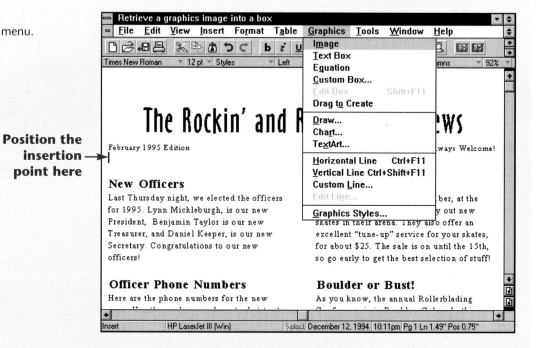

3 **Choose Custom Line.**

The Create Graphics Line dialog box appears (see Figure 6.12). You use this dialog box to specify options for a horizontal or vertical graphic line. By default, you create a horizontal line running from the left to the right margin.

4 **Click the Line Style button.**

This action opens a palette of custom line styles (see Figure 6.12).

Figure 6.12
The Create Graphics Line dialog box with the custom line styles palette displayed.

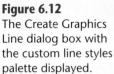

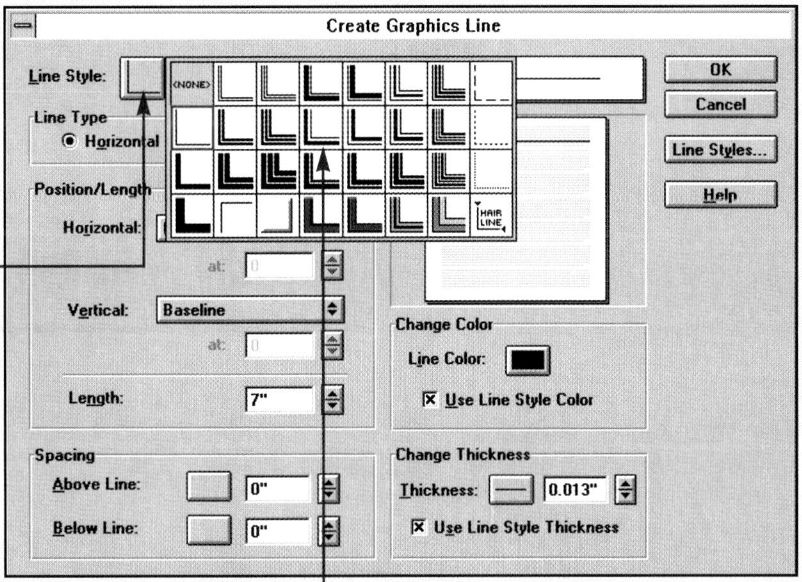

Click this button to open the pop-up box of line samples

Click here to choose the Thick/Thin 2 style

⑤ Click the Line Style button in the 4th column, 2nd row.

The **L**ine Style text box should now have the Thick/Thin **2** style in it.

If you have problems...

If you have problems selecting the correct line style, click the drop-down arrow next to the **L**ine Style text box; then select Thin/Thick **2** from the drop-down list. You have to scroll through the list to see this option.

⑥ Choose OK.

Choosing OK inserts the horizontal line. The newsletter should now look like Figure 6.13.

continues

To Insert a Graphic Line (continued)

Figure 6.13
The newsletter masthead with the graphic line.

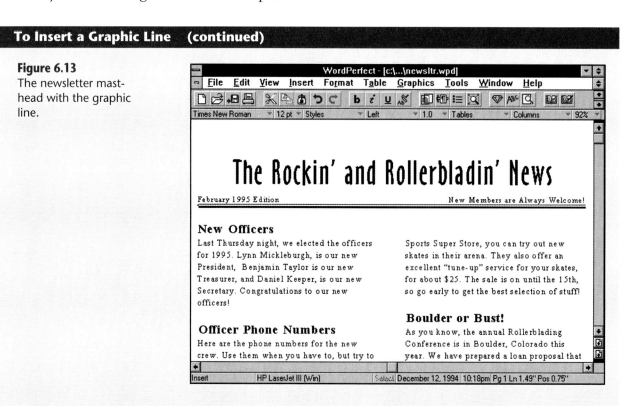

Save your work and keep the NEWSLTR.WPD file open to use in the next lesson, where you learn to insert a graphic image into your document.

Lesson 6: Inserting a Graphic Image

WordPerfect has incorporated mid-level desktop publishing tools into the program since the early DOS versions of the program. As a matter of fact, the graphics box, which enables you to include clip art, scanned art and photographs, charts, text, and equations in your documents, was a revolutionary feature. Although WordPerfect has its own graphics format (WPG), it also accepts other commonly used graphic formats such as PCX, TIF, PIC, and EPS, among others.

WordPerfect still uses a graphic box to insert graphic images into a document. You can resize the graphic, and the box can be positioned virtually anywhere in a document. You can even change the outside border of a graphic box to frame the graphic image. Try inserting a graphic image into the newsletter now.

To Insert a Graphic Image

❶ **In the NEWSLTR.WPD file, position the insertion point at the beginning of the paragraph under the heading Boulder or Bust!**

You want to insert the graphic box here.

② **Choose Graphics, Image.**

The Insert Image dialog box appears. In most cases, the WordPerfect for Windows Graphics directory already appears. If that directory doesn't appear in your dialog box, use the drive and directory lists (or the QuickList entry, if you have one) to locate this directory of graphic files. WordPerfect includes over 100 graphic files that you can use in your documents.

③ **Select the INKSKIER.WPG file from the Filename list box; then choose OK.**

WordPerfect inserts the image in its original size at the insertion point. The text of the paragraph has been formatted to wrap around the box. Solid squares, called *sizing handles*, appear on all sides of the box. You learn about these handles in the next lesson. In addition to the handles, a Graphics feature bar appears at the top of the document window (see Figure 6.14).

Figure 6.14
This graphic box contains the INKSKIER.WPG file.

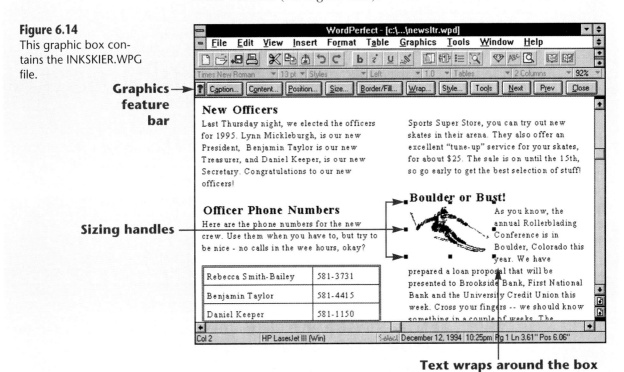

Graphics feature bar

Sizing handles

Text wraps around the box

Save your work and keep the NEWSLTR.WPD file open to use in the next lesson, where you learn to move and resize a graphic image.

To Move and Resize a Graphic Image (continued)

Figure 6.16
The text of the paragraph wraps around the graphic box.

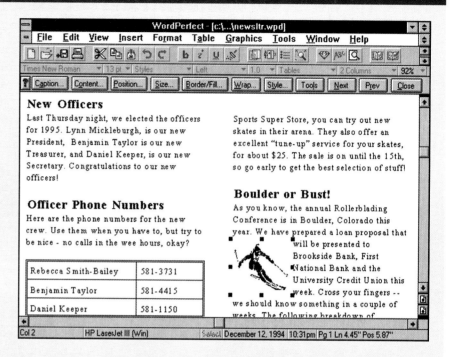

7 Click inside the document window to deselect the graphic and remove the sizing handles.

The changes you have made to the sample newsletter in this project have improved the quality of this important document. Save your work and print two copies of NEWSLTR.WPD, one to keep and one to turn in. Close the document after printing. If you have completed your session on the computer, exit WordPerfect for Windows and the Windows Program Manager before turning off the computer. Otherwise, continue with the "Applying Your Skills" case studies at the end of this project.

Jargon Watch

In WordPerfect, a **graphics box** enables you to insert a variety of graphic elements into a document by placing a graphics box in the document and then inserting the graphic image into the box.

Sizing handles are small squares on a picture border that you use to size a picture. Clicking and dragging a sizing handle increases or decreases the size of the graphic box.

When you hear someone refer to text **wrapping** around a graphic box, that term indicates that the text surrounds a graphic box.

You can use the buttons on the Graphics feature bar to change the size and position, as well as the contents (if you decide you want to use another image) of a graphic. If you want to frame the image, you can use the Border/Fill button to choose a border style and a fill style (like a shaded background). The Wrap button tells WordPerfect how you want the text to wrap around a graphic box. In addition, you can use the WPDraw applet, a full-scale drawing program that allows you to create your own drawings from scratch, to edit a graphic image.

Checking Your Skills

True/False

For each of the following statements, check *T* or *F* to indicate whether the statement is true or false.

__T __F **1.** The Table Expert has a series of styles that you can choose from to change the number style used in a table.

__T __F **2.** Tables can format text and numbers into columns.

__T __F **3.** The spreadsheet functions in WordPerfect have similar capabilities as those seen in powerful spreadsheet programs.

__T __F **4.** Graphic boxes enable you to insert clip art images into a document.

__T __F **5.** The results of a formula appear in a table cell, not in the calculation itself.

Multiple Choice

In the blank provided, write the letter of the correct answer for each of the following.

1. You can place _____ in a graphic box.

    a. clip art

    b. equations

    c. scanned photographs

    d. all the above

2. The most commonly used calculation in Tables is _____.

    a. Present Value

    b. Future Value

    c. Square Root

    d. Sum

3. A _____ graphic line stretches from the left to the right margin.

    a. vertical

    b. custom

    c. horizontal

    d. marginal

4. In a table, pressing ⇧Shift + Tab⇄ moves you _____.

    a. one cell to the right

    b. one cell to the left

    c. to the top cell of a table

    d. to the bottom cell of a table

5. The WordPerfect graphics files have the _____ extension.

    a. PCX

    b. WGF

    c. WPG

    d. EPS

Completion

In the blank provided, write the correct answer for each of the following.

1. _____ lines frequently separate letterhead, masthead, headers, and footers from the rest of the text.

2. WordPerfect includes _____ files that you use to enhance your documents.

3. A table _____ is the intersection of a row and a column.

4. The cell address is composed of the column _____ and the row _____.

5. You can resize a graphic box with sizing _____.

Applying Your Skills

Take a few minutes to practice the skills you have learned in this project by completing the "On Your Own" and "Brief Cases" case studies.

On Your Own

Create a Party Invitation

Now that you have spent some time working with WordPerfect's Tables and Graphics features, you can create an invitation for a card party you plan next weekend for the Rollerblading Club. Club members will provide the following food and drinks: pizza, salad, bread sticks, brownies, cookies, and soft drinks. Use a table to list the members who are bringing food and drinks along with the menu items each person will provide. Insert a picture from the WordPerfect clip art to liven up the invitation.

To Create the Invitation

1. Open a new document, and create a large heading using one of the decorative fonts included in WordPerfect.

2. Insert a horizontal line; then customize the line with one of the line styles.

3. Type a greeting; then list the items you will serve at the party. Use a different font for this text.

4. Type a short paragraph introducing the table that lists the guests and the food items they have agreed to bring. Ask guests to bring additional decks of cards for card games.

5. Create a table with the names of the members and the food items they have agreed to bring.

6. Use the Table Expert to assign an informal style to the table.

7. Using the clip art files of your choice, create two graphic boxes within the invitation.

8. Resize and move the graphic boxes to position them where you want them to appear.

9. Save the invitation as **CLUBINV.WPD**; then print two copies of it.

Brief Cases

Create a Company Newsletter

Use the skills you have learned in this project to create a company newsletter for the employees of Sound Byte Music. Include information about new releases, new employees, and plans for a company picnic. Create a table listing the top ten sellers for the previous month. Create another table listing new employees and their telephone numbers. Insert at least one picture to "spice up" the newsletter.

To Create the Newsletter

1. Open a new document, and then create a heading using one of the decorative fonts included in WordPerfect.

2. Use a smaller font size to enter the date of the newsletter and the company name. Position the date flush left and the company name flush right.

3. Insert a custom horizontal line—choose one of the predefined styles.

4. Start with information on new releases. In this section, type a short introductory paragraph for the Top Ten table.

5. Create a table for the Top Ten Sellers of last month. Create columns for (1) This week's number, (2) Title, and (3) Last month's position on the chart.

6. Type in the ten best selling albums/cassettes/CDs.

7. Use the Table Expert to format the Top Ten table. Choose an informal, flashy style.

8. Type a paragraph or two describing plans for the company picnic next weekend. Give the time and location.

9. Type a short paragraph introducing three new employees.

10. Create a table for the names of new employees and their phone numbers. Include at least three employees.

11. Choose a graphic image and insert it into a graphic box in the document. Depending on the image you have chosen, size and position the box in the newsletter.

12. Save the file as **COMPNEWS.WPD**, and print two copies of it.

Project 7

7

Using Merge

Setting up a Mail Merge

In this project, you learn how to
- Create a Data File
- Enter Information into a Data File
- Create a Form File
- Create an Envelope Form File
- Merge Files

Why Would I Do This?

When you want to send a personalized letter to a number of people, you can use WordPerfect's Merge feature. Consider the cover letter that you created in Project 2. If you need to send your resume out to a number of people, you can save time by setting up the cover letter as a form file and then merging in the names and addresses of the recipients. The result, a personalized letter, gives the impression that you typed each letter individually. In reality, you only typed the letter once.

For this project, you send out a notice to all the members of the Rollerblading Club. Using the notice as your sample document and the instructions provided in this project, you learn how to use the Merge feature to create a notice and an envelope for each club member.

Lesson 1: Creating a Data File

There are two types of files in a merge: a *data file* and a *form file*. The data file contains the name and address information. The form file is the document you want to send out to everyone—in this case, the notice. You can have multiple form files in a merge. For example, a typical mail merge has a letter and an envelope form file.

The first step in creating the data file is deciding how you want to organize the information. For example, you can keep all the name information together, or you can break it into first name and last name. Separating the first name and last name enables you to use the first name and the last name separately in the form document.

Follow the steps below to create a data file for the members of the Rollerblading Club. You need to start from a blank document window, so if necessary, save and close any documents on-screen.

To Create a Data File

❶ In a new, blank document, choose Tools; then choose Merge.

The Merge dialog box appears (see Figure 7.1). The Merge dialog box is used to create the data and form files and to merge the two files.

Figure 7.1
The Merge dialog box.

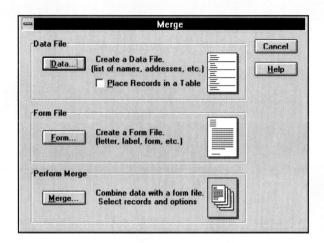

> ② **Choose Place Records in a Table.**
>
> This action tells WordPerfect to create a table for the data file information. You can enter the data file information into the document window or into a table, a much easier task.
>
> ③ **Click the Data button.**
>
> The Create Data File dialog box appears (see Figure 7.2). In merge files, each piece of information is called a *field*. You use this dialog box to tell WordPerfect what fields you want to have in your data file.

Figure 7.2
The Create Data File dialog box.

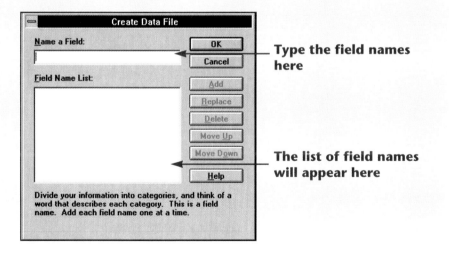

Type the field names here

The list of field names will appear here

> ④ **Type First Name in the Name a Field text box, and press** ⏎Enter.
>
> WordPerfect places First Name at the top of the **F**ield Name List list box.
>
> ⑤ **Type Last Name in the Name a Field text box, and press** ⏎Enter.
>
> Last Name now appears as the second field name in the list.

continues

To Create a Data File **(continued)**

❻ Type Address in the Name a Field text box, and press ⏎Enter.

A field can be any length, so you can use one field for the street address, no matter how many lines it takes.

❼ Type City in the Name a Field text box, and press ⏎Enter.

In this example, the city, state, and zip code information are separated into three fields. Mail merges often use this kind of separation because you have the option of sorting (arranging) by city, state, or zip code. In order to qualify for discount postal rates, for example, your mail has to be sorted by zip code.

❽ Type State in the Name a Field text box, and press ⏎Enter.

WordPerfect places the field name "State" in the Field Name List list box.

❾ Type Zip in the Name a Field text box, and press ⏎Enter.

You have now completed the list of fields for the data file. The Create Data File dialog box should now look like Figure 7.3. Verify that your list matches the one shown in this figure before you move on to the next step.

Figure 7.3
The Create Data File dialog box with all the field names.

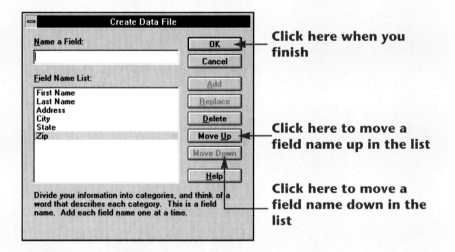

If you have problems...

If your fields aren't in the right order, or if you accidentally skipped a field, you need to take care of it now. If you forgot to insert a field name, do it now. Select the new field name; then use the Move **U**p option to insert it in the correct place in the list. The Move D**o**wn option moves a selected item down through the list. Continue selecting field names and moving them until they are listed in the correct order.

⑩ Choose OK.

WordPerfect creates the data file table, and then displays the Quick Data Entry dialog box, where you will enter the name and address information for the club members in the next lesson (see Figure 7.4). Make sure you leave this dialog box open for the next lesson.

Figure 7.4
The Quick Data Entry dialog box with all the field names.

Click here to move the insertion point down a field

Click here to move the insertion point up a field

Quick Data Entry	
Record	Next Field
First Name	Previous Field
Last Name	New Record
Address	Close
City	Delete Record
State	Find...
Zip	Field Names...
	Help
First Previous Next Last	

Click here when you finish

Press Ctrl+Enter to add a new line at the insertion point.
☐ Edit Fields with Functions

Jargon Watch

In WordPerfect, you work with two files in a merge—the data file and the form file. A **data file** contains the information that will be inserted into the form file (names, addresses). The **form file** contains the information that doesn't change from one person to the next (letter, notice, invitation). When you create the form file, you insert markers where you want to insert information from the data file.

In a data file, each piece of information is called a **field**. You can have an unlimited number of fields. A **record** is a collection of all the fields for an individual. You can have as many records in the data file as you need.

Lesson 2: Entering Information into a Data File

One of the benefits of creating the data file for the Rollerblading Club members is that you can use it again if you need to send another mailing or create a roster of your members.

In the previous lesson, you defined the fields in the data file. In this lesson, you type the name and address information into the fields you defined using the Quick Data Entry dialog box. Try entering the information now.

To Enter Information into a Data File

❶ In the Quick Data Entry dialog box, type Heather in the First Name field text box, and press [↵Enter].

The Quick Data Entry dialog box should be open on-screen from the preceding lesson. If not, click the **Q**uick Entry button on the Merge feature bar to open the Quick Data Entry dialog box. Pressing [↵Enter] after typing in a field moves you to the next field.

If you have problems...

If your Quick Data Entry dialog box doesn't match the one shown in Figure 7.4, you can choose Field N**a**mes to switch to the Edit Field Names dialog box. In this dialog box, you can edit field names and rearrange their order in the list.

❷ Type West in the Last Name field text box, and press [↵Enter].

Remember, you only need to enter the last name here.

❸ Type 1603 Laurel in the Address field text box, and press [↵Enter].

In this case, the address is only one line long. A field can, however, have as many lines as you need. The scroll bars for the field text box enable you to scroll through a multi-line field.

❹ Type Edford in the City field text box, and press [↵Enter].

You have just entered the city name. Remember, you enter the state and zip code information in separate fields.

❺ Type Indiana in the State field text box, and press [↵Enter].

❻ Type 46033 in the Zip field text box.

This action enters the information for the last field of the record. Your information in the Quick Data Entry dialog box should match Figure 7.5.

Figure 7.5
The Quick Data Entry
dialog box with the first
record entered.

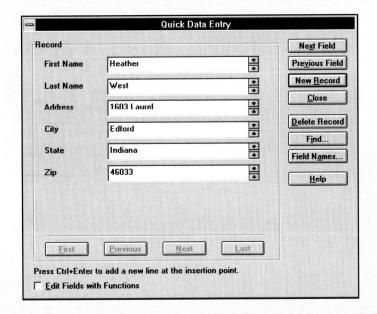

If you have problems...

Before you press ⏎Enter in the last field, look back through the information you have typed and make sure it is correct. If you made a mistake while entering the information, you can correct it before you save the information to disk. Use the **F**irst, **P**revious, **N**ext, and **L**ast buttons at the bottom of the Quick Data Entry dialog box to move between the records. The Pre**v**ious Field and Ne**x**t Field buttons move you through the fields in a particular record.

❼ **Press** ⏎Enter.

Pressing ⏎Enter in the last field takes you to a new blank record.

❽ **Using the preceding steps, enter the following names in the Quick Data Entry dialog box:**

continues

To Enter Information into a Data File   (continued)

Jeffery Andrews **1105-B Jimmy Drive** **Bloomington, Indiana 46032**	**Benjamin Taylor** **4801 Allen Street** **Apt. 603** **Nashville, Indiana 46037**
Lynn Mickleburgh **432 Greenlee** **Apt. 1601** **Martinsville, Indiana 46030**	**Daniel Keeper** **Jackson Hall** **2nd Floor South** **Bloomington, Indiana 46032**
Chuck Sharon **708 West Gibson** **Greenwood, Indiana 46293**	**Patty Clark** **8405 Jelson Blvd.** **Edford, Indiana 46055**

When you have two lines in the address, press Ctrl+⏎Enter to move to a new line in the field.

❾ Choose Close.

WordPerfect closes the Quick Data Entry dialog box and asks you if you want to save the changes to disk.

❿ Choose Yes.

Choosing Yes opens the Save Data File As dialog box (see Figure 7.6). You need to type a name for your data file so that WordPerfect can save the information you entered.

Figure 7.6
The Save Data File As dialog box.

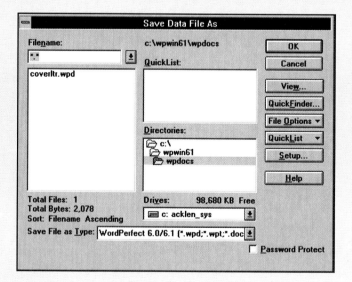

⓫ Type clublist in the Filename text box, and choose OK.

WordPerfect saves the file automatically with a DAT extension, which identifies the file as a data file.

A table with the name and address information now appears in the document window. The Merge feature bar displays under the Power Bar to assist you while you work with merge documents (see Figure

7.7). Don't worry about the way the text wraps inside the table cells—this won't affect the way the text appears when you merge. If you prefer, you can adjust the column widths and format the table, but you don't have to go to the trouble.

Figure 7.7
The data file table with the name and address information.

Merge feature bar

Click here to return to the Quick Data Entry dialog box

Click here to open the Merge dialog box

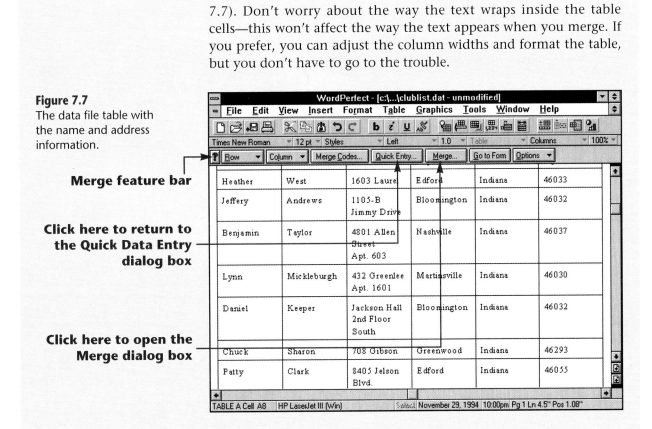

⑫ **Choose File, Close.**

This action closes the CLUBLIST.DAT document. If you made any changes since you last saved the file, WordPerfect prompts you to save those changes. In the next lesson, you learn how to create a form file.

Lesson 3: Creating a Form File

In a merge, the form file contains the information that stays the same for all the recipients—in this case, the notice you plan to send out to the members. You insert field codes where you want information from the data file to appear. These codes match the field names you used in the data file. When you merge the two documents together, WordPerfect matches up the field codes with the field names and inserts the information.

You can either create a form file from an existing document, or you can start from scratch. In this case, the notice you want to send out has already been created, so you open that document and insert a field code for the members' first names.

To Create a Form File

❶ Open the PROJ0701.WPD file, and save it as CLUBMTG.WPD.

You will send out this notice to the club members. Because the notice has an informal style, the greeting after the heading reads Hey -. You need to insert a field code for the member's first name between Hey and the dash. You only need this piece of information from the data file for this form document. The rest of the information will be used in the envelope form file.

❷ Choose Tools, Merge.

The Merge dialog box appears. You use the Merge dialog box to create the form file.

❸ Choose Form.

If you have a document on-screen, the Create Merge File dialog box appears.

❹ Make sure Use File in Active Window is selected; then choose OK.

Choosing OK opens the Create Form File dialog box (see Figure 7.8). You use this dialog box to tell WordPerfect which data file goes with the form file you are creating.

Figure 7.8
The Create Form File dialog box.

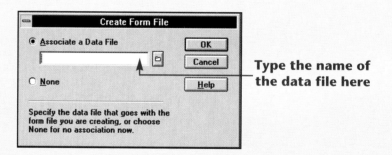

Type the name of the data file here

❺ Type clublist.dat in the Associate a Data File text box.

WordPerfect assigns an extension of DAT to all data files when you save them, so you need to use this extension when you type the data file name.

❻ Choose OK.

WordPerfect creates an association between these two files so that the next time you open this file, WordPerfect knows which data file to use with this form file. A Merge feature bar has been added to the document window (see Figure 7.9).

Click here to insert a field code in the document

Figure 7.9
The Merge feature bar
has buttons that give
you access to merge
features.

Merge feature bar

**Position the insertion
point here**

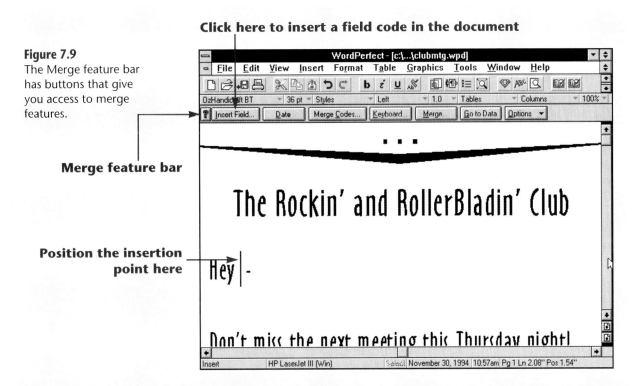

7 Position the insertion point between Hey and the dash that follows.

You insert the field code for the club member's first name here.

8 Click the Insert Field button on the Merge feature bar.

The Insert Field Name or Number dialog box appears with a list of the field names you created in the CLUBLIST.DAT file. Because the First Name field name is the first in the list, it already appears selected.

9 Choose Insert.

The First Name field code is the word "Field" with the field name in parentheses (see Figure 7.10).

10 Choose Close.

Choosing Close clears the Insert Field Name or Number dialog box. Because you only need the First Name field code, you have finished creating the form file. The notice should now look like Figure 7.10. Save your work in the CLUBMTG.WPD file, and leave this document open so that you can use it in the next lesson.

continues

To Create a Form File (continued)

Figure 7.10
The notice file with the
First Name field code.

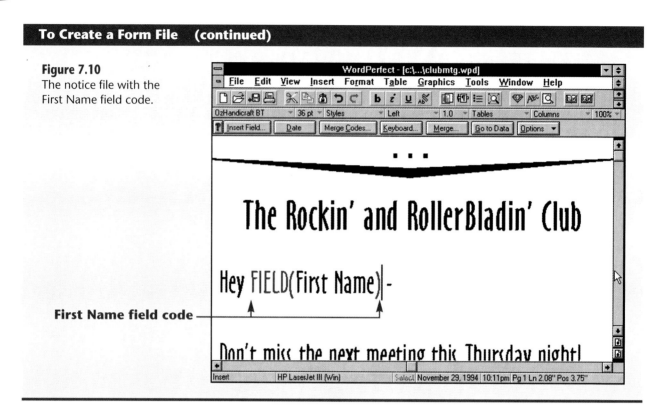

First Name field code ————

Lesson 4: Creating an Envelope Form File

Because you want to mail the meeting notices to all club members, you create and attach an envelope form file to the notice form file, which enables you to merge the two form files with the data file at the same time.

The envelope form will contain field codes for the members' names and addresses. Try creating an envelope form file now.

To Create an Envelope Form File

❶ Click the Merge button on the Merge feature bar.

The Merge dialog box appears.

❷ Choose Merge.

The Perform Merge dialog box appears (see Figure 7.11). You create the envelope form from this dialog box. By default, WordPerfect is set up to merge the current document with the data file you specified earlier.

❸ Choose Envelopes.

The Envelope dialog box appears (see Figure 7.12). Use this dialog box to insert your return address and the field codes for the member information.

Figure 7.11
The Perform Merge
dialog box.

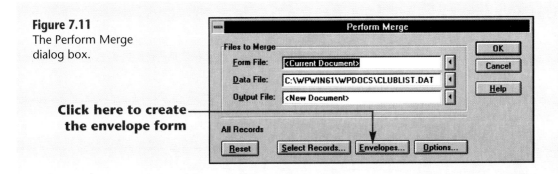

**Click here to create
the envelope form**

**Type your return
address here**

**Insert the field
codes here**

Figure 7.12
The Envelope dialog
box.

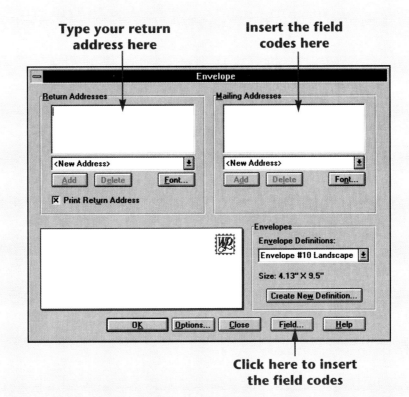

**Click here to insert
the field codes**

❹ **Type the following address in the Return Addresses text box:**

Megan L. Taylor

11050 Park Lane Avenue

Carmel, Indiana 46032

As you type your return address, it appears on the sample envelope
in the dialog box.

❺ **Click the Mailing Addresses text box.**

Clicking the **M**ailing Addresses text box places the insertion point
inside the text box. You insert the field codes for the name and
address information from the data file here.

continues

6 Choose Field.

The Insert Field Name or Number dialog box appears. You used this same dialog box earlier to insert the First Name field code in the notice form file.

7 Choose Insert.

The First Name field code is the first field code in the list, so it already appears selected for you. You will need to select the other field codes before you can insert them.

8 Press the Spacebar once.

You need to insert a space between the First Name field code and the Last Name field code. You place all spacing and punctuation in the form file, not the data file.

9 Choose Field, and select the Last Name field code; then choose Insert, and press ⏎Enter.

Because the street address should appear on a separate line, you need to press ⏎Enter before inserting the Address field code.

10 Choose Field, and select the Address field code; then choose Insert, and press ⏎Enter.

Here again, you want the city-state-zip information on a separate line, so you need to press ⏎Enter before inserting those field codes.

11 Choose Field, and select the City field code; then choose Insert.

12 Type a comma and a space.

It's customary to have a comma followed by a space between the city and state, so you have inserted those items into the envelope form.

13 Choose Field, select the State field code, and then choose Insert; press the Spacebar twice.

It's also customary to have two spaces between the state and zip code.

14 Choose Field, select the Zip field code, and then choose Insert.

The Envelope dialog box should now look like Figure 7.13.

15 Choose OK.

WordPerfect clears the Envelope dialog box and takes you back to the Perform Merge dialog box. Notice the message displayed on top of the buttons—All Records; Envelopes. This message indicates that you will merge all the records in the data file and that you have attached an envelope form file to the notice form file. Make sure you leave the Perform Merge dialog box open so you can perform the merge in the next lesson.

Figure 7.13
The Envelope dialog box with the field codes in the Mailing Addresses text box.

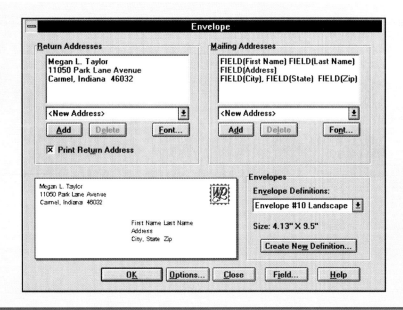

Lesson 5: Merging Files

After you create the form files and data files, you merge the files together—the easiest part of the entire process. When you merge the files, WordPerfect looks through the form file for field codes and then matches these codes with the field names in the data file. When a match is found, WordPerfect pulls the information from the data file and inserts that information into the form file.

Because a new copy of the form is created for each record in the data file, you will have seven copies of the notice form and seven copies of the envelope form. Try merging the files now.

To Merge Files

❶ In the Perform Merge dialog box, choose OK (refer to Figure 7.11).

WordPerfect displays a Please Wait message box that shows the progress of the merge. When the merge is complete, the insertion point appears at the bottom of the last notice.

❷ Position the insertion point at the top of the document.

The notice should now look like Figure 7.14. Notice that the first name has replaced the field code.

continues

Figure 7.14
The notice after the merge.

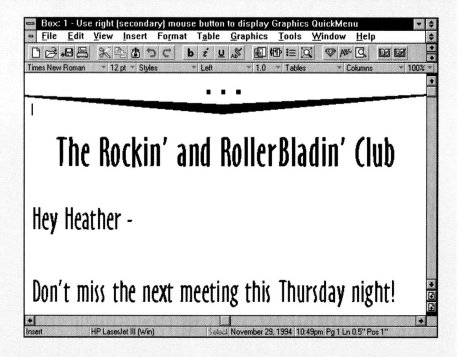

❸ **Click the Zoom button on the Power Bar, and choose Full Page.**

Choosing a Zoom setting of Full Page displays the entire page on-screen so that you can see how the notices and envelopes will look when printed.

❹ **Press Alt+PgDn.**

Pressing Alt+PgDn moves you to the next page in the document. You can continue pressing Alt+PgDn to view each of the notices and the envelopes. The envelopes contain all of the information from the data file, so check these carefully to make sure everything appears in the right spot.

 ❺ **Click the Print icon.**

Clicking the Print icon opens the Print dialog box.

❻ **Choose Print.**

Choosing Print sends the notices and the envelopes to the printer. The notices print first, followed by the envelopes. Most printers accept envelopes through a manual feed tray, so be ready to insert envelopes into the printer, if available. If you don't have envelopes, print this information on regular paper.

❼ **Double-click the document Control-menu box.**

Double-clicking the Control-menu box closes the document window. WordPerfect prompts you to save your changes.

❽ Choose No.

In most cases, you don't need to save the results of a merge because you can merge the two files again later.

> **If you have problems...**
>
> If the results of the merge are not what you intended, just close the document that contains the results of the merge, make the necessary corrections in the data and form files, and then perform the merge again.
>
> First, make sure you didn't delete part of the field code—the parentheses and the word "Field" are very important. If you have deleted any part of the field code, delete the rest of the code, and then re-insert the code. You can't type these codes from the keyboard.
>
> Second, make sure you included the correct spacing and punctuation in the form file. All spacing and punctuation should be included in the form file, not the data file.
>
> Third, make sure the field names in both files match exactly. If they don't, WordPerfect will not insert the information in the form file.

❾ Double-click the document Control-menu box for the CLUBMTG.WPD document.

This action closes the form file. If you have made any changes since you last saved the file, you will be prompted to save your changes. Choose **Yes** to save the file.

The results of the merge will be sent to a new document. Each of the three options under the Files to Merge section can be modified by clicking the arrow button next to the text box and selecting from the drop-down list.

If you prefer, you can choose to send the results of the merge to the current document window, directly to the printer, or to a file that you could print later. In the Perform Merge dialog box, click the arrow next to the Output File option, and choose from the drop-down list it displays.

Checking Your Skills

True/False

For each of the following statements, check *T* or *F* to indicate whether the statement is true or false.

__T __F **1.** Field names in both the form file(s) and the data file must match exactly.

__T __F **2.** The form file contains the information you insert into the data file.

__T __F **3.** The Quick Data Entry dialog box lets you enter the field names you want to use in the data file.

__T __F **4.** Each piece of information in the data file is called a record.

__T __F **5.** You can create a form file from scratch or from an existing document.

Multiple Choice

Circle the letter of the correct answer for each of the following.

1. Which of the following should be used as a file name for a data file?

    a. BLACKTOP.WPD

    b. BLACKTOP.DAT

    c. MEMBERSHIP.DAT

    d. MEMBERS.DOC

2. What is it called when you "tie" a data file to a form file?

    a. an association

    b. a file connection

    c. a merge

    d. a file relationship

3. When you insert a field code into a form file, it looks like _____.

    a. F (First Name)

    b. Field [First Name]

    c. FIELD (First Name)

    d. FIELD {First Name}

4. You can create an envelope main document from the _____ dialog box.

    a. Create Form File dialog box

    b. Perform Merge dialog box

    c. Quick Data Entry dialog box

    d. Merge dialog box

5. You must define the _____ before you can enter information in the data file.

    a. field codes

    b. field names

    c. data fields

    d. merge codes

Completion

In the blank provided, write the correct answer for each of the following statements.

1. When you merge a data file with a form file, a new form is created for every _____ in the data file.

2. The _____ file contains field codes where the information from the data file will be inserted.

3. You can create both data and form files from the _____ dialog box.

4. You can have as many _____ in a record as you need.

5. You can merge different _____ files with the same data file in a merge.

Applying Your Skills

Take a few minutes to practice the skills you have learned in this project by completing the "On Your Own" and "Brief Cases" case studies.

On Your Own

Creating a Mail Merge with Your Resume Cover Letter

Now that you have learned some basic skills with WordPerfect's Merge feature, create your own merge for your resume cover letter. Do this by creating a short data file with the names and addresses of prospective employers. Then, open the cover letter and modify it by adding field codes where the names and addresses should be inserted. Also create envelopes with the field codes for the names and addresses.

To Create the Merged Cover Letter

1. Create a data file with the following names and addresses. When you create the data file, be sure you create a field for the company name. Also, create a field for a salutation (i.e. Mr. College) for each individual.

Mr. Chris College **Seatek Enterprises** **100 Elm Street** **Indianapolis, IN 46032**	**Ms. Mary Spangler** **Taylor Homes** **100 West 5th** **Carmel, IN 46290**
Ms. Lynn Stewart **Emily Sayer Enterprises** **8701 North IH-43** **Bldg. 6, Suite 11** **Indianapolis, IN 46032**	**Mr. Bill Jelson** **Advanced Data Systems** **Cross Road Business Park** **1100 Jackson Blvd.** **Indianapolis, IN 46290**

2. Save the data file as **LETTRLST.DAT,** and close the document.

3. Open the PROJ0702.WPD file, and save it as **COVRLTR2.WPD**.

4. Instruct WordPerfect to create the form file with the file in the active window.

5. Create the association between the LETTRLST.DAT data file and the revised cover letter.

6. Replace the name and address with field codes for the names and addresses in the data file.

7. Create an envelope form with fields for the names and addresses.

8. Merge the cover letter and envelope forms with the data file.

9. Save your work on the COVRLTR2.WPD file, and print the results of the merge.

Brief Cases

Create a Mail Merge for the Radio Ad Copy

Use the skills you have learned in this lesson to set up and execute a merge that will produce a cover letter to be sent out with the ad copy you created in Project 2. You need to define and fill in a data file for the names and addresses of the local radio stations that will broadcast your advertisement. Then, prepare a short cover letter with field codes for the name and address information. Create an envelope form with field codes for the name and address information.

When these files have been saved, merge them together to produce personalized cover letters and envelopes for your ad copy.

To Create the Personalized Cover Letter

1. Define a data file with field names for name, company, and address information. You should probably include a formal salutation.

2. Type in several names and addresses for local radio stations (KLBJ, KEYI, and KBTO).

3. Save the data file as **RADIOLST.DAT**.

4. Open the file PROJ0703.WPD, and save it as **RADIOLTR.WPD**.

5. Insert field codes for the name and address information.

6. Create an envelope form file.

7. Merge the cover letter and envelope form files with the data file.

8. Save your work on the RADIOLTR.WPD file, and print the results of the merge.

Using Macros and Templates

Automating Your Work

In this project, you learn how to

- Record a Macro
- Play a Macro
- Play a WordPerfect Shipping Macro
- Use a WordPerfect Template

Why Would I Do This?

Macro
A series of actions that can be defined, recorded, and used again later.

Now that you have seen the variety of tasks you can perform in WordPerfect, you may want to know how you can make these tasks faster and easier. Although some word processing tasks only require a step or two, others require a series of steps, which means you spend a lot of time making selections from the menus and dialog boxes. WordPerfect gives you a way to speed up these tasks—a *macro*.

Macros are small computer programs that you can write in WordPerfect to speed up repetitive tasks. Using your own name and address information and the instructions provided in this project, you learn how to record a macro that types your return address for you. You then play the macro in a sample document. Finally, you play the letter macro that comes with the WordPerfect program.

Template
A document that contains boilerplate text and formatting.

WordPerfect provides another feature to help you automate your work—templates. A *template* is a document with built-in formatting—you just fill in the information. WordPerfect includes a large selection of professionally designed template documents for your use. In this project, you use a fax cover sheet template to create a cover sheet.

Lesson 1: Recording a Macro

Creating a macro in WordPerfect is like making a tape recording. When you record a song with a tape recorder, you insert a tape, press Record, and record the song as it plays on the radio. When you want to listen to the song again, you insert the tape, press Play, and listen as the song plays from the tape.

Play
To execute a macro. Playing a macro is the same as "running" a macro.

When you create a macro in WordPerfect, you record your actions (keystrokes and commands). For example, you can record a macro for typing your company name, inserting a horizontal graphic line, or setting up the format for a formal report. *Playing* a macro is simply playing back the actions you recorded. Virtually anything you can do in WordPerfect can be done using a macro.

To Record a Macro

1 Using a new document, choose Tools, Macro.

The **M**acro submenu appears (see Figure 8.1).

2 Choose Record.

The Record Macro dialog box appears (see Figure 8.2). You need to assign a name for your macro now. A macro name can have up to eight characters. WordPerfect automatically assigns an extension of WCM to its macros. Don't type another extension, or WordPerfect will not recognize the file as a macro.

3 Type retadd.

WordPerfect records the macro in the file RETADD.WCM.

Figure 8.1
The **M**acro submenu.

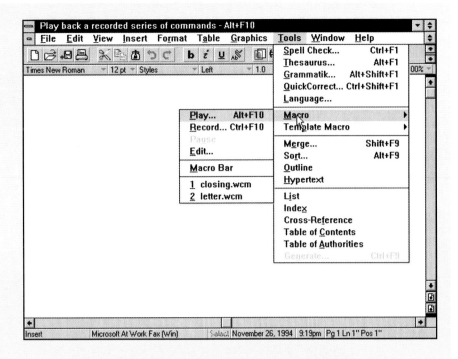

Figure 8.2
The Record Macro
dialog box.

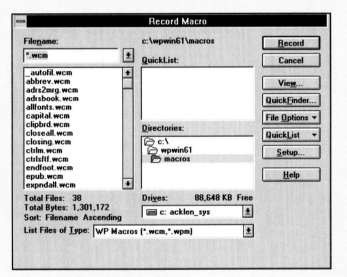

4 **Choose Record.**

The Record Macro dialog box closes, and you are returned to the document window. The Macro feature bar appears under the Power Bar (see Figure 8.3). You are now in the Macro Record mode.

While inside the document window, the mouse pointer displays as a circle with a line through it, which means you can't use the mouse in the document window. (You may recognize the circle as the international symbol for *no*.) The mouse *can be* used in the menus and dialog boxes; consequently, when you move the mouse pointer to the menu bar or to a dialog box, the normal mouse pointer reappears.

continues

To Record a Macro **(continued)**

Figure 8.3
A sample return
address.

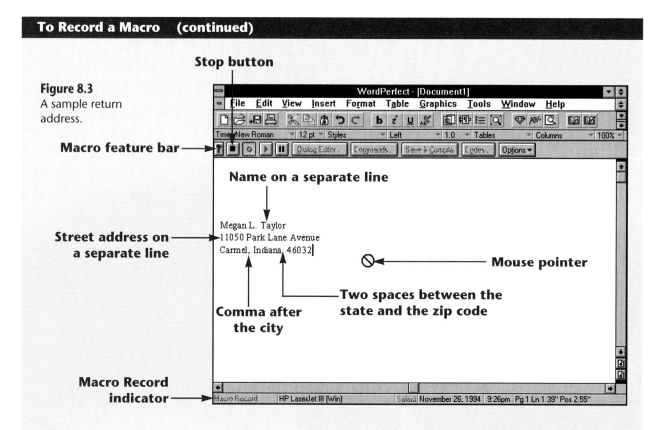

⑤ **Type your name and address.**

You should type your name and address as you want them to
appear when you play the macro in a letter or envelope document.
Traditionally, your name and street address appear on separate
lines; your city, state, and zip code information appear on the same
line. See Figure 8.3 for a sample return address.

If you have problems...

If you make a mistake, don't worry about it—just backspace over
the mistake and type the correct information. The macro plays so
quickly that you probably won't see any of your extra steps.

When you record a macro, don't include unnecessary insertion
point movement. For example, if you press Ctrl+Home before
you type your return address while recording the macro, the
macro performs that keystroke when it runs. If you have included
unwanted insertion point movement actions in the macro, stop
recording the macro (see the following steps), and start over.

When you finish, you need to turn off the macro recorder. If you forget to turn the recorder off, WordPerfect continues to record keystrokes until you exit the program or turn the recorder off.

6 Choose Tools; then choose Macro.

Notice that the Record option has a check mark next to it, indicating that the recorder is on.

7 Choose Record.

When you choose Record, it deselects the Record option, which turns off the macro recorder. The Macro feature bar disappears off the screen and the regular mouse pointer displays in the document window. When you turn the recorder off, WordPerfect saves the macro to the file name you gave the macro earlier.

You may want to insert a couple of blank lines between the return address you just typed and the one that the macro types into the document in the next lesson. If you prefer, you can close this document without saving the changes.

You can click the buttons on the Macro feature bar rather than selecting from the menus to perform common macro tasks. For example, you can click the Stop button to stop the playing or recording of a macro (see Figure 8.3).

Learn to record macros any time you are performing a repetitive task in a document. It's easy to record a macro as you are performing a task, such as adding a date to a letter. Just use the steps described in this lesson. The keystrokes you enter then serve two purposes—entering text into a document and recording a macro you can use over again later.

Lesson 2: Playing a Macro

Now that you have recorded your macro, you are ready to play (or run) it. The WordPerfect installation program creates a MACROS directory and copies the macros that come with the program into that directory. Any macros that you create will also be stored in this directory, which makes locating your macro files easier.

What is a Computer Program?

A computer program is simply a list of commands that tells the computer how to perform a task. The commands tell it where to take the input from, how to process it, and what kind of output goes where.

In essence, by recording a simple macro as you do in this project, you act as a computer programmer. The actions you record in your macro become the steps of a short and simple computer program.

Some computers, like the one in a digital watch, have all of their programs built-in. You can't change the program to make the watch do anything but tell time. The only commands that you can give the watch are the few that the built-in program was designed to understand.

Personal computers, however, are designed to let you put in different programs. Just like a VCR can act as a movie theater, an aerobics instructor, or an album of photos of your grandchild (depending on what tape you put into it), a computer can perform many different tasks depending on the programs you install in the computer. When you use a word processing program, the computer becomes a word processor. When you use a game program, it becomes an arcade.

A computer program can be very complex, often involving hundreds of thousands of individual commands. Because a computer only understands a limited (but useful) set of commands, difficult procedures have to be broken into long strings of these small steps.

People who create computer programs (programmers) rarely do so in the language that the computer directly understands (machine language). Machine language commands are nothing but numbers. Instead, programmers write in programming languages designed for programming, which allows them to work in a language that is more understandable to them.

These programs are then translated by another program into a form that the computer can directly handle. These translation programs, called compilers, assemblers, and interpreters, break the big steps of the programming language into the smaller, numeric steps that the computer understands.

Compilers and assemblers translate the program into machine language and save the machine language version on disk. An interpreter handles each of the programmer's commands one at a time, translating each command into the smaller commands the machine understands, and then immediately acting on those commands. Because the interpreter tries to translate the program as well as act on the commands every time the program is used, this process is slower than using a program that has been translated ahead of time by a compiler or an assembler.

*For further information relating to this topic, see Unit 3A, "Software," of **Computers in Your Future** by Marilyn Meyer and Roberta Baber.*

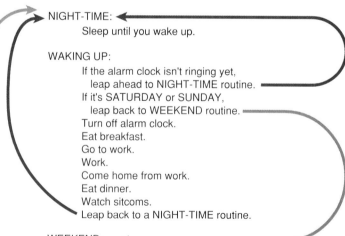

NIGHT-TIME:
　　Sleep until you wake up.

WAKING UP:
　　If the alarm clock isn't ringing yet,
　　　leap ahead to NIGHT-TIME routine.
　　If it's SATURDAY or SUNDAY,
　　　leap back to WEEKEND routine.
　　Turn off alarm clock.
　　Eat breakfast.
　　Go to work.
　　Work.
　　Come home from work.
　　Eat dinner.
　　Watch sitcoms.
　　Leap back to a NIGHT-TIME routine.

WEEKEND:
　　Eat breakfast.
　　Go for a bike ride.
　　Eat lunch.
　　Watch sports.
　　Eat dinner.
　　Watch more sports.
　　Leap back to NIGHT-TIME routine

To Play a Macro

❶ From the document in which you typed your name, choose Tools, Macro from the menu bar.

The **M**acro submenu appears.

❷ Choose Play.

The Play Macro dialog box appears (see Figure 8.4). You can either select the macro file from the list, or you can type the name in the File**n**ame text box.

Figure 8.4
The Play Macro dialog box.

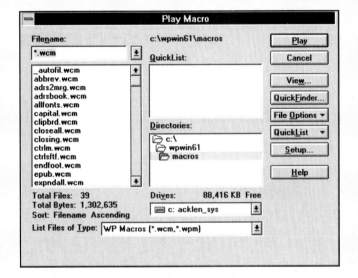

❸ Type retadd.

Notice that you don't have to type the extension for a macro file.

❹ Choose Play.

The macro you recorded plays, entering your return address in the document window. The first time you play a macro, it takes a little longer than the second and subsequent times because WordPerfect translates your keystrokes into program language, which runs faster. Insert some blank lines and run the macro again. Notice how much faster the macro plays the second time around.

Before you go on to the next lesson, close the document without saving your changes—this was only for practice.

WordPerfect remembers the last four macros that you play and it lists them at the bottom of the Macro menu (see Figure 8.5). If you use the same three or four macros consistently, you can save a few seconds by selecting them from the bottom of the Macro menu rather than going into the Play Macro dialog box.

In the preceding lesson, you typed the name of the return address macro; then choose **P**lay. You can also click the macro in the list and choose **P**lay, or you can double-click a macro name in the list to play it.

Figure 8.5
The **M**acro menu has a list of the last four macros you played.

List of recently used macros

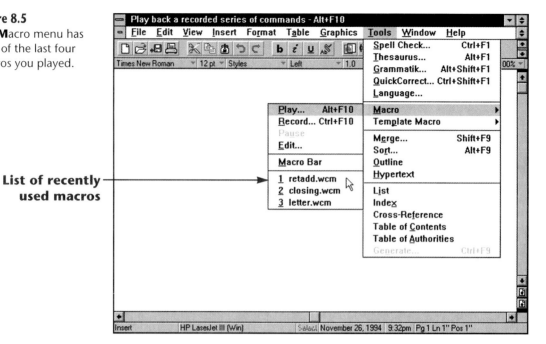

Lesson 3: Playing a WordPerfect Shipping Macro

WordPerfect includes a series of macros with the program called shipping macros. These macros help you perform repetitive tasks and can provide examples if you start writing your own macros.

To access the list of these macros, choose **H**elp, **M**acros; then choose Additional Help, WordPerfect Macros. Selecting this item displays a Help screen with the complete list of shipping macros. If you want to print the list, click the Print button on the Help button bar.

To Play a WordPerfect Shipping Macro

❶ From a blank document window, choose Tools, Macro.

The **M**acro submenu appears.

❷ Choose Play.

The Play Macro dialog box appears. You can either select the macro file from the list, or you can type the name in the File**n**ame text box.

❸ Type letter; then press ⏎Enter].

Remember, you don't have to type the extension when you play a macro file. Pressing ⏎Enter] after typing the macro name is probably the fastest method of executing the macro, but you can choose **P**lay if you prefer.

The Personalize Your Templates message box appears if you (or anyone else) has not yet entered the personal information that WordPerfect uses in certain macros and templates (see Figure 8.6).

Figure 8.6
The Personalize Your
Templates message
box.

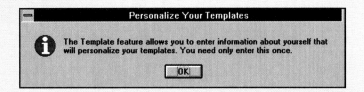

If you have problems...

If you are working in a computer lab, someone else may have already entered this information. In that case, WordPerfect skips the message box, and opens the Letter dialog box. Choose **P**ersonal Info to open the Enter Your Personal Information dialog box so that you can add your information.

4 Choose OK.

The Enter Your Personal Information dialog box appears (see Figure 8.7).

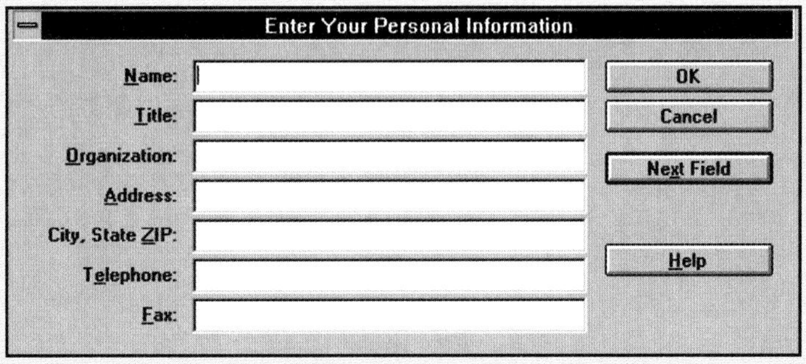

Figure 8.7
You use this information with many macros and templates.

Enter Your Personal Information	
Name:	OK
Title:	Cancel
Organization:	Ne**x**t Field
Address:	
City, State **Z**IP:	
T**e**lephone:	Help
Fax:	

5 Enter your personal information, pressing `Tab↕` **or** `↵Enter` **to move down to the next text box.**

If the text box has someone else's personal information, select the text first; then enter your information to replace the previous text.

6 Choose OK.

The Letter dialog box appears (see Figure 8.8). The insertion point already appears in the **R**ecipient's Name and Address text box, so type that information now.

continues

Figure 8.8
Use the Letter dialog box to type the necessary information.

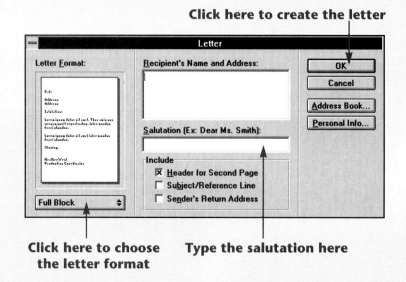

Click here to create the letter

Click here to choose the letter format

Type the salutation here

7 **Type the following name and address:**

> **Mr. Chris Twins**
> **Senior Partner**
> **Taylor and Andrews**
> **103 First Street**
> **Indianapolis, IN 46263**

You have just provided the name and address of the individual you are sending the letter to, so make sure the information is correct.

8 **Click the Salutation text box.**

Clicking the Salutation text box moves the insertion point into the text box.

9 **Type Dear Mr. Twins:.**

By default, the Letter macro inserts a header on the second page of the letter. If you prefer to use a subject/reference line or to insert your return address in the letter, make sure you check the appropriate check box in the Letter dialog box to select those options.

10 **Choose OK.**

Choosing OK runs the rest of the Letter macro, which inserts the information into a new document window (see Figure 8.9).

Now that you have created the letter form, you can now enter the body text for the letter. Because you are just practicing, you don't need to fill in the letter now. Close the document without saving before you begin the next lesson, where you learn how to use the WordPerfect templates.

Figure 8.9
The letter macro inserts the date, the name/address, and salutation for you.

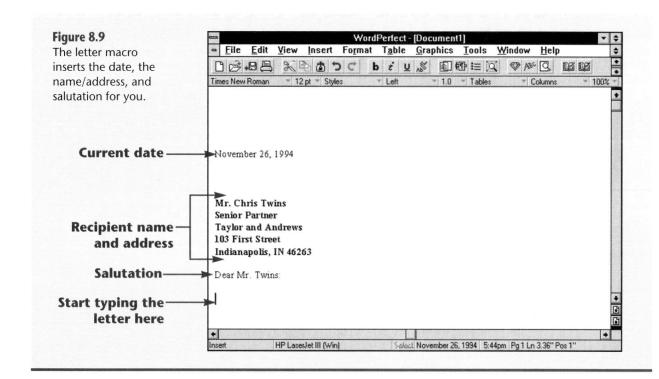

Current date ——▶ November 26, 1994

Recipient name —— ▶ Mr. Chris Twins
and address   Senior Partner
                       Taylor and Andrews
                       103 First Street
                       Indianapolis, IN 46263

Salutation —— ▶ Dear Mr. Twins:

Start typing the —— ▶
letter here

In the Letter dialog box, you can choose from four different letter styles by clicking the up/down arrow to open the pop-up list under the letter sample.

If you ever need to edit the personal information, you can play the LETTER macro, choose **P**ersonal Information from the Letter dialog box, and change the information; then choose Cancel in the Letters dialog box (canceling the macro so you don't create a letter now).

You may want to use another shipping macro, called CLOSING. The closing macro has a selection of 13 different closing phrases that you can use to close your letters.

Lesson 4: Using a WordPerfect Template

In the projects in this book, you have had the opportunity to see some of the most commonly used formatting commands, so you should have an appreciation of the effort it takes to create a properly formatted and professional-looking document. By using the predefined document templates that come with WordPerfect, you can eliminate much of the time and effort in creating common types of documents. These templates are predefined documents with all the formatting built in—you just fill in the blanks and print.

WordPerfect includes a wide variety of templates, from desktop publishing documents to calendars to legal briefs. One of the most frequently used form documents is a fax cover sheet. Try filling out the template for a fax cover sheet now.

To Use a WordPerfect Template

① In a blank document window, choose File, New.

This action opens the New Document dialog box, which allows you to select a template to use for the new document.

② Choose fax in the Group list box.

Choosing fax displays a list of fax cover sheet templates in the Select **T**emplate list box (see Figure 8.10).

Figure 8.10
WordPerfect provides four different fax cover sheets.

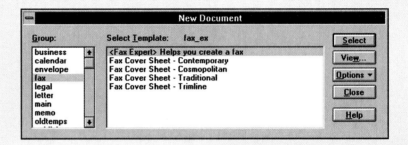

③ Choose Fax Cover Sheet—Trimline.

If you prefer using the keyboard, press ↓ until the Trimline style appears highlighted. You can preview the cover sheet by clicking the Vie**w** button.

④ Choose Select.

Choosing **S**elect opens the Template Information dialog box, where you can type the information for the fax cover sheet (see Figure 8.11). Because you entered your personal information in the Personal Information dialog box earlier in this project, you don't need to enter the information again. That information will be used automatically in the templates where needed.

⑤ Type Mr. Chris Twins.

The insertion point is already in the Name of Recipient text box so that you can type that name as soon as the dialog box opens. Move down to the Fax Number text box by pressing Tab⇥ or clicking the Fax Number text box.

⑥ Type (317) 555-3737.

You type the fax number here; then move down to the Regarding text box.

⑦ Type Jazz Fest.

This information should reflect the subject of the fax and the accompanying documents. Move down to the Pages (including cover sheet) text box.

❽ Type 3.

This number indicates how many pages you plan to send—make sure you add the cover sheet to the page count. Your screen should now look like Figure 8.11.

Figure 8.11
The Template Information dialog box with sample information.

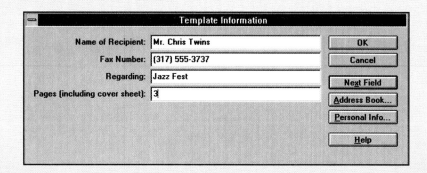

❾ Choose OK.

WordPerfect now switches to the template document and inserts the information you just entered (along with the current date) into the appropriate spots on the fax cover sheet. The personal information appears at the bottom of the page, so you may not see it right away. Your cover sheet should now look like Figure 8.12.

Print/Fax icon

Figure 8.12
The completed fax cover sheet.

Template Toolbar

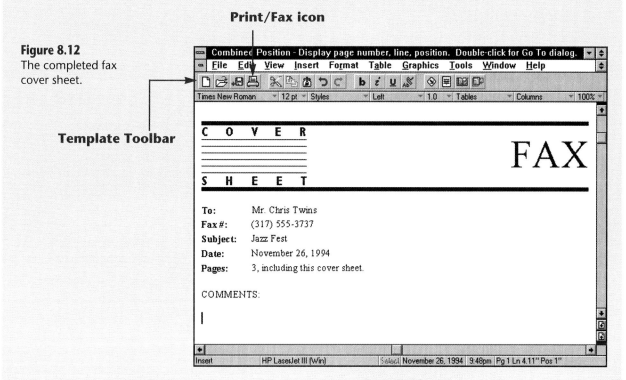

continues

To Use a WordPerfect Template (continued)

Now that you have completed the cover sheet, you can print. Notice that the Toolbar appears in abbreviated form and that the Print icon has changed to the Print/Fax icon. (Point to the icon—note that the QuickTip shows *Print/Fax*.) This Toolbar displays when a template opens. Once the template closes, the regular Toolbar reappears.

⑩ Click the Print/Fax icon on the Toolbar.

⑪ Choose Print to print the fax cover sheet.

If you think you may send fax documents to this recipient again, you should save the completed cover sheet. Otherwise, just close the document without saving. You can always use the template again when necessary.

If you have completed your session on the computer, exit WordPerfect for Windows and the Windows Program Manager before turning off the computer. Otherwise, continue with the "Applying Your Skills" case studies at the end of this project.

If you have a fax board in your computer, you can fax directly from WordPerfect. When you open the Print dialog box, select the fax board as the current printer; then choose **P**rint. WordPerfect then sends the document to the fax. Make sure you switch back to your printer when you finish, otherwise you will send future documents directly to the fax board.

Checking Your Skills

True/False

For each of the following statements, check *T* or *F* to indicate whether the statement is true or false.

__T __F **1.** Creating a macro is similar to recording a cassette tape in a tape recorder.

__T __F **2.** Macro names can be from one to 122 characters.

__T __F **3.** A macro is like a small program that you can write in WordPerfect.

__T __F **4.** You can use the mouse in the document window while recording a macro.

__T __F **5.** You use the Record Macro dialog box to select a shipping macro.

Multiple Choice

In the blank provided, write the correct answer for each of the following.

1. Which of the following is a valid macro file name?

    a. letterclose

    b. header.doc

    c. print.wcm

    d. line.wcm

2. The _____ menu contains the **M**acro command.

    a. **E**dit

    b. F**o**rmat

    c. **T**ools

    d. **I**nsert

3. The four macro files on the Macro menu are _____.

    a. the first four macro files in the Macros directory

    b. the most commonly used macros

    c. the last four macros you played

    d. the last four macros you recorded

4. To play a macro from the Play Macro dialog box, you must _____.

    a. select the macro file from the list; then choose Play

    b. type the name of the macro; then choose Play

    c. type the name of the macro; then press ⏎Enter

    d. all the above

5. A document template is used to _____.

    a. ensure that saved information is stored in memory

    b. display buttons on the WordPerfect toolbar

    c. format the document on-screen

    d. create commonly-used documents with a minimum of formatting

Completion

In the blank provided, write the correct answer for each of the following statements.

1. When you are in Macro Record mode, the mouse pointer displays as a _____.

2. Recording a macro is like recording a _____ with a tape recorder.

3. A macro records your _____, so you can play them back later.

4. The letter macro has a sample page of the _____.

5. Document _____ are documents with the formatting already built-in.

Applying Your Skills

Take a few minutes to practice the skills you have learned in this Project by completing the "On Your Own" and "Brief Cases" case studies.

On Your Own

Creating a Routing Slip Macro

Record a macro that creates a routing slip with the names of the members of the Rollerblading Club. Because you are the club's secretary, you have to distribute newsletters and flyers to the members. The routing slip will consist of a 5-character underscore line followed by a tab, then each member's name. When the member has read the information, they fill in their initials and pass it on to the next member.

To Create the Macro

1. Name a macro with the name **routslip**.

2. Once you turned the recorder on, type the following information:

   _____ **Heather West**

   _____ **Jay Stephens**

   _____ **Kelly Jelson**

   _____ **Jon Crain**

   _____ **Jimmy Gardner**

   _____ **Sharon Orsborn**

   _____ **Chuck Anderson**

3. Turn off the macro recorder.

4. Play the macro.

Brief Cases

Use the skills you have learned in Project 8 to create two macros for Sound Byte Music. The first macro is a memo form from you (the owner) to the employees. The macro types out the memo title and headings. You can enter the subject, date, and memo text later. The second macro is a fax cover sheet from Sound Byte Music to a large radio station (KBIG) that you frequently send faxes to.

To Create the Memo Macro

1. Record a macro called **memoform**.

2. Type the following information:

   ### Sound Byte Music Memo

TO:	Very Cool Sound Byte Music Employees
FROM:	The Boss
DATE:	

3. Turn off the macro recorder.

To Create the Fax Cover Sheet Macro

1. Record a macro called **kbigfax**.

2. Use the Contemporary Fax Cover Sheet template to create the fax cover sheet.

3. Type the following information into the Template Information dialog box:

   Jamie Stewart, KBIG Station Manager
   (513) 555-5251
   New Release from River City Records
   2

4. Turn off the macro recorder.

5. Print the fax cover sheet.

INDEX

The Instructor's Manual includes a Curriculum Guide to help you plan class sessions and assignments. Each chapter in the Instructor's Manual contains teaching tips, answers to "Checking Your Skills" questions, transparency masters, and test questions and answers. The manual also offers suggestions for teaching accelerated classes or students with special needs. Additional project ideas, suggestions, and a data disk containing exercise files are also included.

To order the Instructor's Manual (ISBN: 0-7897-0118-9), please contact your local representative or write to us on school letterhead listing your course number and course name. Use the following address:

S. Dollman

Que Education and Training

201 West 103rd Street

Indianapolis, Indiana 46290-1097